New Zealand

a special place...

New Zealand

a special place...

Lansdowne Press

PHOTOGRAPHERS:
Ray Joyce, Conrad Sims,
Chris Lewis, Logan Murray,
Rodger Grace,
Robert Van Der Voort,
Leonard Cobb

HALF TITLE PAGE:
The tailings left by the gold dredges that worked the
Cromwell Gorge line the banks of the Clutha River.

TITLE PAGE:
Maize fields and kiwifruit orchards tell of the sweeping
changing in agricultural practice in the Bay of Plenty.

END PAPERS:
Sunrise tips the Kaikoura Ranges with their unique
blush.

THIS PAGE:
Dusky Sound in Fiordland, where Captain Cook
spent a month in 1773, reaches back into the lonely
glacier-carved mountains.

Published by Lansdowne-Rigby
A division of Rigby International Ltd
59 View Road, Glenfield, Auckland, N.Z.

© Copyright Lansdowne-Rigby 1986
First published 1986
Research and text by Anna Horne
Editing by Peter Debreceny
Designed by Leonard Cobb Direction Ltd
Typeset by Linoset Services Ltd, N.Z.
                Auckland Typographic Services Ltd
Printed by Everbest Printing Co Ltd, Hong Kong

ISBN 0-86866-088-4

North Island Introduction . . .

In geographic isolation from the major landmasses of the world, washed by the uninterrupted swells of the vast South Pacific Ocean, lie the remote islands of New Zealand. With an economic zone claiming an ocean area six times greater than that of the land, and political responsibility reaching into the tropical heart of Polynesia, New Zealand's island nature is unmistakable.

Geologically New Zealand is a young country; and the North Island is younger than the South. Although the exact nature of the country's beginnings are obscure, it is thought that the very oldest geological components, which date back 600 million years or more to the Pre-Cambrian Age, belonged to the ancient continent of Gondwanaland. Over time scales hard to imagine, Gondwanaland moved and realigned in the process known as continental drift. Vast areas sank beneath the sea, collecting sedimentary deposits that later emerged as sandstones, mudstones and limestones. Other sectors collided and scraped against each other, with the heat and pressure turning the sediments into schists and gneisses. Volcanic activity accompanied the upheavals in the earth's crust and brought igneous rocks — granites, basalts, pumices — from deep within the earth to merge with or lie upon already existing rocks. From the complexities of mountain building and the eras of subsidence emerged the landform we are familiar with today.

The creative processes are still at work. New Zealand is perched on the junction of two of the continental plates. Hot pools and springs of steaming water bubbling through sandy beaches, and occasional earth tremors, evidence this throughout the North Island. However, it is at the thermal wonderlands of Rotorua and Taupo that the earth's raw energy is seen at its most spectacular. Boiling mud pools plop alongside long-playing geysers; silica terraces display the colours of the rainbow; mineral baths soothe with healing salts. Active volcanoes are a further feature of the thermal activity that brings tourists from all over the world. In the sweeping arc of the Bay of Plenty, White Island sends up a constant cloud of steam. To the south-west, 175 km from Rotorua, the graceful mountains of Tongariro, Ngauruhoe and Ruapehu rise beyond Lake Taupo. Amidst the snow, hot springs and steaming crater lakes exist. The classic shape of Ngauruhoe betrays this mountain's continual volcanic activity, and as recently as 1975 the mountain erupted, showering trampers in the area with scoria. Ruapehu, the North Island's principal alpine resort, has also surprised skiers by gushing lava down its slopes!

The North Island landscape is studded with reminders of its recent geological past. Vast Lake Taupo fills a crater formed by the world's largest rhyolitic eruption in the second century A.D. Further north, the city of Auckland is built upon numerous volcanic cones, and the gracious island of Rangitoto emerged a mere 800 years ago.

Of the origins of New Zealand's earliest settlers, the Moa Hunters (named after the large flightless bird, now extinct, that was their main food), little is known. Then, so the myths say, some thousands of years ago, Polynesians from Hawaiki set sail in open, ocean-going canoes, bound for a land their legendary navigator Kupe had discovered far to the south. Aotearoa, he had called it: 'Land of the Long White Cloud'. Weeks of hardship and sheer endurance passed before these brave travellers sighted White Island's rising steam, the beacon that would guide them into the open embrace of one of Aotearoa's most benign regions. Later, Captain James Cook would name it, aptly, the Bay of Plenty. The new immigrants to these shores settled extensively along the coast of the North Island, apart from the inhospitable Wairarapa region in the south-east. Some tribes followed the path of thermal activity inland to utilise the hot pools for cooking and warmth. The fertile banks of the natural canoe highways, the Waikato and Wanganui Rivers, provided good ground for the kumara (sweet potato) brought down from the tropics, and these became highly populated areas.

On the East Coast they found hospitable bays, lagoons and harbours, a coastline protected by offshore islands — as in the Hauraki Gulf and the Bay of Islands. Currents and winds from the north brought the warmth of the tropics. The sea abounded with fish, the bush-clad coast with birds. On the other hand, the west coast from Ahipara at the end of Ninety Mile Beach to the plains below the Wanganui River was an ungiving, wild, elemental place constantly under attack from the prevailing southwesterlies and a storm-whipped sea. Settlements were centred on the large, protected harbours with mangrove-lined tidal waterways, concealed behind towering sand dunes and narrow entrances.

Te Ika a Maui, 'The Fish of Maui', is the traditional name for the North Island. Was it the extensive travelling of the newcomers around the land, or some wider perception, that influenced their myths and explanations of the origins of Aotearoa? Cast your eye over the map of the North Island . . . now hear the story.

Way back in the mists of time, Polynesian demi-god Maui and his brothers paddled far from their homeland of Hawaiki in search of a good catch. Unbeknown to the others, Maui's fish-hook was made of an enchanted bone, and the fish it snared was so heavy Maui had to sing a magic chant to ease its weight. The brothers were filled with jealousy at his success.

'Wait!' Maui bade them. 'Wait! I must fetch the tohunga (priest) to remove the sacred tapu on this special catch.'

But the brothers couldn't wait. They beat the huge fish to kill it and began hacking away at its flesh. It writhed in agony beneath their blows, and their disrespect angered the gods. That is why the North Island is scored by hills and mountains, and in places the great fish writhes still.

Now look again at the map. Beyond the canoe of Maui — the South Island — is a lifeless fish. The mouth can be seen in the indentation of Wellington Harbour, an eye at Lake Wairarapa. Fins spread out at East Cape and Taranaki and a tail stretches to the north! Even the hook remains to this day, embedded in the curve of Hawke Bay.

The first European to see New Zealand was the Dutchman Abel Tasman, who made his landfall off the West Coast of the South Island in 1642. His only contact with the 'natives' was a bloody confrontation at what is today called Golden Bay. From there he sailed north, making sketchy charts and naming the tip of the North Island Cape Maria van Diemen and the islands beyond, the Three Kings. His visit lasted less than a month, and it was not until more than a century later that the British ship *Endeavour*, captained by James Cook, sighted the east coast in 1769.

Cook's journals of this first circumnavigation, along with those of two further voyages, aroused European interest. His reports of the Coromandel and Northland kauri forests rapidly brought timber traders keen to exploit the large stands for spars and ship building. In the Manawatu, traders exchanged firearms for flax and shrunken heads. The Bay of Islands quickly became a busy home port for whalers and sealers, although, with rowdy grog shops, whore houses and skittle alleys, it also gained a reputation as the 'Hell Hole of the South Pacific'!

The European arrivals became known as Pakeha, or 'foreigner', and in turn the indigenous peoples united under the appellation of Maori, an adjective from their language meaning 'ordinary' or 'normal'.

The effect of pakeha traders on the Maoris was dramatic and terrible. As Captain Cook had observed, the native people indulged in a highly developed system of intertribal warfare that encompassed an unforgiving concept of revenge — utu. Once the traders' muskets intruded on a system formerly regulated by hand-held weapons, the loss of life in battle increased. This, combined with the ravages of previously unknown diseases, resulted in the Maori population being decimated.

Missionaries arrived, distressed by the influence of the traders on the locals, and also driven by their religious zeal. Humanitarians stirring at home in England, the missionaries already in New Zealand, a threat that France would claim sovereignty, and pressure from companies keen to colonise the land for their own economic gain were all factors that led to Britain's decision to annex New Zealand.

In 1840 the historic Treaty of Waitangi was signed. In the heat of a Northland summer day, Lieutenant-Governor William Hobson and a number of Maori chiefs put their marks to a paper declaring British sovereignty.

For forty years, battles flared throughout the North Island as tribes who had not been signatories to the treaty resisted pakeha demands for land and others discovered fraudulent sales.

Unifying elements emerged: the Maori King Movement and several religious and pacifist leaders, most notably Te Whiti, who led the final resistance at Parihaka Pa in Taranaki in 1881. With the loss and confiscation of so much of their land, the spirit of the Maori people suffered terribly. It was to take the efforts of three Young Maori Party statesmen, Ngata, Pomare and Buck, in the opening decades of the twentieth century, to rekindle Maori pride.

Once New Zealand had been declared a British colony, many immigrants began to make the long sea voyage from Europe to their land of new prospects. English settled at Auckland, New Plymouth, Wanganui and Wellington. Irish came out to special settlements in the Bay of Plenty. Dalmations and Yugoslavs were attracted to the gumfields in the north. Hardworking Scandinavians opened up the bush lands north of Wellington.

Timber was cleared from the hills, gold mined from the Coromandel range, and throughout the country pastures of sheep and dairy cattle appeared. Within 130 years, two-thirds of the original forest, tussock and scrub had been converted into farmland, and New Zealand had won herself the title of Britain's farm of the South Pacific.

The latter half of the twentieth century has seen a reappraisal of New Zealand's traditional links with Britain. Successive generations are barely aware of ties to 'Mother' England any more.

Economically, England's entry into the E.E.C. has encouraged the development of new markets, diversifying the traditional farming culture, with much grazing land being converted to horticulture. The Bay of Islands and the Bay of Plenty, subtropical in climate, now grow exotic fruits like tamarillo, kiwifruit, passionfruit and babaco. In the Waikato and Hawke Bay vineyards abut dairy farms. Even the pine forests are diversified with blackwood, gum, walnut and kauri trees. Experimental crops of nuts, soya beans and even rice are being grown.

Prompted by the oil crisis of the 1970s, a desire for self-sufficiency in fuel, steel and manufactured goods has affected the nature of industry.

Commendably, while the people of this land tend to concentrate in the cities, particularly in those of the northern half of the North Island, there is a noticeable conscience shown towards the natural environment. North Islanders love water sports, outdoor living, fresh air, and the chance 'to get away from it all' in the weekends.

But, as much as the wonderful diversity of landscape, the attraction of the North Island lies in the inter-mingling of South Pacific cultures: European, Maori, Pacific Islander and Asian.

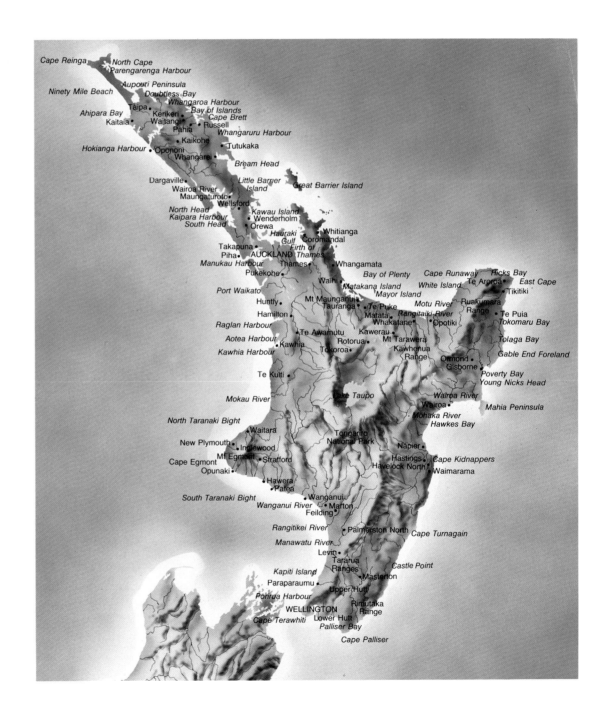

CAPE REINGA Into a confusion of wave and current caused by the meeting of the Tasman Sea with the Pacific plunge the northern extremes of the New Zealand coast. The mood of Reinga belongs to Maori legend. From here the spirits of the departed begin their long journey of return to the traditional homeland of Hawaiki, far away in the mystical beginnings of Polynesia. An ancient and weathered pohutukawa clinging to the cliffs above the breakers guides the spirit to the gap in the swirling kelp which is the door to the underworld.

Since 1941, the steep volcanic ridgeline of the cape has been dominated by the white lighthouse, providing its own beacon for seafarers.

NINETY MILE BEACH This remarkable beach stretches the entire western length of the narrow spit which links Cape Reinga with Kaitaia. For 90 kilometres it follows an almost straight line broken but once by the isolated 'Bluff' until it reaches the small Maori community of Ahipara.

WAIPAPAKAURI A wooden ramp at Waipapakauri gives one of the few useful vehicle accesses to Ninety Mile Beach. Once the area was the site of a major gumfield, now local people have established the country's first community forest.

WHANGAROA HARBOUR The scallop shells on the tidal mangrove flats of Whangaroa Harbour hint at the rich sea life found in the area, ranging from shellfish and crayfish to the big game prizes — mako sharks, marlin and tuna.

TAUROA POINT Old Pa sites on the hills of Tauroa Point forming the southern boundary of Ahipara Bay tell of the large Maori population of the past.

The Maori saw the West Coast as fierce and masculine. The half submerged remains of the "Favorite" which foundered in 1870 in Wreck Bay in this vicinity are a reminder that this coast offers no shelter in a storm.

KERIKERI nestles on one of the Bay of Islands' many inlets, providing a meeting place of past and present. The charming Old Stone Store built in 1833 continues to serve the local community and the nearby Kemp House, built from pit sawn timber, is the oldest house in the country. Aptly, the town's name translates as 'keep on digging'. The pocket of rich volcanic soil here combined with the mild 'winterless North' climate is highly productive. The local Ngapuhi had cultivations of kumara growing here when Samuel Marsden and the first missionaries arrived in the early 1800s. In 1920 the first citrus orchards were laid out, and now the area supplies New Zealand with half of its sweet citrus fruit. Other subtropical fruits with export potential, kiwifruit and tamarillo, are also being planted.

THE KAURI (Agathis australis), a conifer native to New Zealand, is the 'King' of the northern bush, occurring naturally from the Waikato northwards. Initial growth of rickers (the saplings are named after naval 'riggers') is rapid but maturity is not reached for hundreds of years. Then the tree may stand for over a thousand.

The mature tree has a crown of many branches tipped with thousands of tiny spiked leaves, rising majestically above the rest of the forest.

POMPALLIER HOUSE The missionaries brought literacy to the Maori. Pompallier House was built to accommodate the Roman Catholic mission's printing press in 1841-42, though Bishop Pompallier never actually lived there — its name was bestowed by a resident in 1931.

Forest King. . .

THE KAURI STORY Captain James Cook noted these superb trees as he sailed along the Northland and Coromandel coasts in 1769 and recognised their value as sailing ship spars. By 1800 they had become a trading commodity between the Maoris and whalers, although not without bloodshed at first. The Europeans lacked the Maoris' reverent attitude for the living forest and conflict was inevitable when customs and tapus were transgressed, albeit usually unwittingly. But by 1820, the Maori had joined forces with the Pakeha. Millions of feet of timber were hauled by bullocks over log skid roads to bustling ports which had sprung up on every northern harbour. Down chutes and streams the logs were channelled for export to Sydney and England.

Within a hundred years the region was all but denuded of trees. Had it not been for an upsurge of public concern in the early 1950s even the Waipoua State Forest, the last virgin kauri forest of any significant size, may have fallen. This reserve, along with the smaller Trounson Kauri Park Sanctuary, has about half of the 10,000 hectares of mature forest that remain out of the original three million hectares of kauri bush.

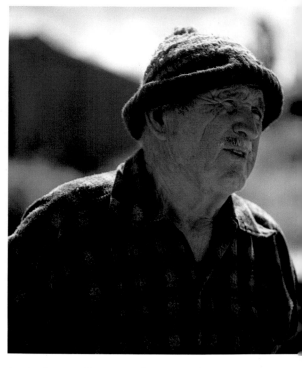

As the forests disappeared a new trade developed: kauri gum. The Maoris had used it for chewing gum and black stain tattooing. Its many hues of amber and brown, polished up and sometimes with insects and plants preserved within, had long given it value to collectors. But the commercial value lay in its hardening and gloss qualities. Until synthetics were developed, varnish, paint and linoleum industries paid high prices for this resin.

It lay beneath the swamplands of the Aupouri Peninsula and still flowed, lifeblood, in the remaining kauris. Many of the surviving trees show scars from where they were gashed and bled until the practice was declared illegal.

At Houhora and Ahipara big communities of gumdiggers, swollen by many immigrants from Dalmatia (today's Yugoslavia), sprang up. The diggers probed the swamps and scrubland with sharp "gum spears" to locate the lumps of gum, fossilized remnants of ancient forests. Their endeavours brought a second round of wealth to the North.

At Ahipara the Historic Places Trust has preserved one of the last gumfields of the 1930s. There can be seen the scars left as vast tracts of land were dug and divided by the gumdiggers' searching trenches.

WHANGAROA KAURI MILL A stack of swamp kauri awaits dressing. The grey colour of the wood indicates it has probably been dug out of a bog or recovered from where it has lain for many years in the bush. The natural resin of the timber has preserved it, even though many years have passed since it was a growing tree. Kauri's resistance to rot, its long straight grain and golden colour have made it a highly prized material for yacht construction and furniture making.

Lane's Timber Mill is the most famous of Northland's few remaining kauri sawmills and well known to boatbuilders as far away as Auckland. It dates back to 1872 when as Lane and Brown's Shipbuilding Yard it contributed to Whangaroa's early coastal trading fleet.

Land of contrasts. . .

WEST COAST NORTH OF KAIPARA The Maoris saw the West Coast of Northland as male by nature and here in this ungiving, abrupt meeting of sea and land it is easy to see why. Gone are the gentle nurturing inlets of the female East Coast a mere 45 kilometres away — this is a savage coast laid bare by westerly storms from the Tasman Sea. The long empty beaches are relieved only by the occasional headland such as the Maunganui Bluff pictured here, or the dunes at the entrances to the few harbours.

EAST COAST, NORTH OF WHANGAREI From Bream Head, at the entrance to Whangarei Harbour, to Cape Brett, the beginning of the Bay of Islands, the East Coast is highlighted by scores of exquisite white sand beaches. There are several sheltered harbours offered by the irregular coastline, and one, Tutukaka Harbour, is base for an active big game fishing fleet.

Bountiful Sea. . .

MATAURI BAY 'Million Dollar View Road' is the name given to the road that winds down the saddle to Matauri Bay, an appropriate description for the panoramic vista out to the Cavalli Islands. Captain Cook named them thus after receiving a gift of fish from the local Maoris and the waters are as rich with sealife as ever. For those who are keen underwater divers, the Cavallis are a well known attraction. If you're staying on the shore, a dig in the sands at low tide is bound to yield enough pipis or tuatuas for a good feed.

THREE KINGS ISLANDS AND POOR KNIGHTS Misty on the horizon from Cape Reinga lie the Three Kings Islands. Some 250 km further south-east cluster the Poor Knights. The former were named by Abel Tasman who, anchoring here on the Epiphany in 1643, commemorated the Magi of biblical times. Less royally, it has been suggested the Poor Knights were named by Cook in 1769 after an English recipe/pudding of that name!

Both groups feature steep cliffs rising abruptly out of deep waters and both are washed by the sub-tropical East Auckland Current. This very saline and warm current has its origins off the East Australian Coast and as such extends a special influence on the marine life of the Three Kings and the Knights. Tropical fish species are carried down to the New Zealand coast and many survive in the luxuriant marine environments of the islands. Corals, too, grow well in the confines of the abnormally high water temperatures and coral gardens dotted with brilliantly coloured sponges can be found by divers below the kelp zone.

The sport of scuba diving attracts increasing numbers each year. The marine reserve of the Poor Knights has over 50 named diving spots and, with its proximity to the edge of the continental shelf, a particularly wide range of diving possibilities. Not surprisingly this popularity supports New Zealand's largest fleet of dive charter boats. While the Three Kings boast caves and a wide variety of fish, their distant and exposed situation gives rise to strong currents and rips making their marine treasures far less accessible.

Both island groups are scenic reserves and cannot be landed on without a permit.

GULLS Seabirds are prolific in the Hauraki Gulf. The Gulf Maritime Park extends over 13,000 sq. km and presents a wide variety of protected habitats for many species of birds. Red billed and black-backed gulls like these circling Neverfail Rock breed prolifically throughout the gulf. The adolescents, brown plumaged, vie with the mature gulls for fish or, where there are people, foodscraps. Noisy scavengers these. The white-fronted tern, symbol of the Park is New Zealand's commonest sea swallow. Locally it is known as the 'kahawai bird' for where those fish are, there too are the terns. And soon after, the fishermen, guided by the birds working above the school.

TUATARA Tuataras link the contemporary world with the age of the dinosaurs. Called living fossils, these famous reptiles are found only in New Zealand. They probably arrived from South America via Antarctica when New Zealand was still part of a large southern continent. While elsewhere this prehistoric creature died out at least 60 million years ago, inexplicably they survived on coastal islands near the Hauraki Gulf in the north and in the Marlborough Sounds in the south.

CUVIER ISLAND A solitary island rises, fortresslike, off the tip of the Coromandel Peninsula. Since 1889 the Cuvier Island lighthouse has guided shipping from the south and east to the Colville Channel, and thence to the safe waters of the Hauraki Gulf. Among the early lighthouse keepers, the Cuvier light was considered the worst posting of all. Not only were mails and supplies notoriously irregular, at times even the carrier pigeons refused to fly off into the high winds that buffeted the island.
The lighthouse has recently been automated and the rugged Cuvier is being left as a scientific reserve within the Hauraki Gulf Maritime Park.

POOR KNIGHTS Twisted limbs of pohutukawa (Metrosideras excelsa) wind their way out of a tangled coastal scrub of flax and pohuehue. Fully adapted to local conditions of strong winds and salty sea spray, (the name means 'spray-sprinkled'), the pohutukawa forests of the Poor Knights have been regenerating strongly in the two hundred years since the Ngati Wai sub-tribe abandoned its village here. The undergrowth, protected by the dense canopy of leaves, hosts a myriad of fascinating animals and insects. Flax snails, giant centipedes and bush wetas, and the legendary tuataras happily live in corners such as this.

25

GREAT BARRIER ISLAND When the hurricane season renders sailing in the tropics dangerous, many cruising yachts make their way further into the South Pacific. New Zealand features some of the best sailing in the world and in the summer months many foreign yachts are found in her waters.

Here, in one of the numerous sheltered inlets on Great Barrier Island, a visiting yacht swings safely at anchor.

Smokehouse Bay on Aotea (the Maori name for this large island protecting the entrance to the Hauraki Gulf) has been a particularly favourite spot for several generations of yachties. For here they can fire up a wetback stove to heat water from a nearby stream and plunge into a deep steaming hot bath. There's now a makeshift shed of corrugated iron for privacy put up in later years by the prudent officers of the Spirit of Adventure, but the original flax bush screen is still there. Tubs for washing clothes and clotheslines have also found their way to this informal and welcome facility.

MIMIWHANGATA At Mimiwhangata Farm Park in Northland, people, as well as sheep and cattle, have right-of-way. This recent addition to New Zealand's park system is the result of a novel decision. When Lion Breweries, one of the country's giant business houses, cancelled plans to develop a tourist resort on this attractive headland it was put in trust for the use of all and is now jointly administered with the Hauraki Gulf Maritime Park.

Mimiwhangata's 800 hectares at the southern end of Whangaruru Harbour are a tantalizing medley of East Coast farmland, two sand beaches and over 100 archeological sites. Once large Maori pas here offered refuge to local hapus (tribes). Today picnickers travel from as far as Auckland for the park's fishing, surfing, walking and fresh air

KAWAU ISLAND The scenic Kawau Island with its historical Mansion House is one of the most popular recreational islands in the Hauraki Gulf. Boaties flock to the sheltered waters and in summer the many bays are crowded with yachts. Day trippers have access by ferry from Sandspit, a short 8 kilometres away.

Earliest inhabitants were the shark fishing Ngati Wai and Ngai Tai tribes. Thirteen pas (fortified villages) have been identified but these keen fighting people had quit the island by 1826.

Soon after, Kawau became the site of New Zealand's first industry. Copper was mined successfully until 1855 when sea water flooded the shafts and stopped the operation.

Governor Sir George Grey, owner of Kawau between 1862 and 1888, was responsible for creating the unique environs of Mansion House Bay. He introduced exotic trees and plants from throughout the world — oaks, olives, palms and rhododendrons — and planted pine forests. This diverse vegetation hosts a variety of birdlife including the colourful rosella parakeets and noisy kookaburras he released. Wallabies, too, survived.

Grey's home, the stately Mansion House, carefully restored to its original condition, is open to visitors.

KOLA DANCERS, DARGAVILLE These Kola dancers in their colourful embroidered costumes bring a Mediterranean atmosphere to the Kaipara Harbour. Their forebears were lured to the kauri gumfields of Northland around 1900. When the gum ran out these same Dalmatians turned to dairy farming, especially in the Dargaville area. Others established vineyards on the banks of the Wairoa River and at Henderson, just west of Auckland. The annual wine harvesting festivals are fine opportunities for traditional Yugoslavian dancing and celebration.

Puhoi, a small mixed farming area just north of Auckland, was settled by hardy pioneers from Bohemia in 1863. Isolation and language barriers helped preserve their Germanic traditions. Bohemian dances and customs remain part of local life and visitors to the 'Puhoi Pub' are reminded of the ethnic origins of the small settlement by the photographic display on the walls. Immigrants such as these have added to the predominantly British heritage imposed by the early colonists a cosmopolitan variety.

New Zealand Christmas tree. . .

WENDERHOLM Wenderholm Reserve, 50 km north of Auckland on the Hibiscus Coast, is one of the regional Parks administered by the Auckland Regional Authority.

It encompasses a bush-clad headland with walking tracks to views of the Hauraki Gulf, dropping down to a safe surf beach backed by a pohutukawa fringed picnic spot. Safe boating and swimming make this a perfect family retreat from the city.

POHUTUKAWA The pohutukawa is New Zealand's 'Christmas tree'. Its rich red blooms enflame the coastline with colour in December, and the earlier they bloom, the longer and hotter the summer, it is said. This native seems to flourish and survive in the most difficult conditions. To crumbling cliffs, isolated islands of rock, windswept shorelines the gnarled grey roots cling tenaciously and somehow draw sustenance from salt-tainted soils.

WHANGAPARAOA Nine cities lie within the greater Auckland region to cover an area larger than Paris or Rome. Here at the Whangaparaoa Peninsula north of Auckland, farms and holiday beaches have become commuter suburbs. An efficient and ever expanding network of motorways links them with other parts of this highly mobile city.

POHUTUKAWA Caught in the fiery hues of the setting sun, a gaunt pohutukawa keeps vigilant watch over a sheltered bay.

LANGS BEACH Every New Zealander holds a brilliant tableau of summer holidays within his memories of childhood. In years to come, these youngsters, too, will look back on this sparkling day and fondly remember how hot the white sand was, how warm the Pacific waves were, how few clouds blocked out the sun.
Langs Beach, 50 km south of Whangarei, is a popular East Coast beach.

City of sails. . .

Auckland's waterfront has undergone many changes in the 150 years
since Governor Hobson bought 3000 hectares from the local Ngati
Whatua and proclaimed Auckland the new capital of New Zealand. The
first British immigrants had to wade ashore from their ships. The original
wharves were flimsy and unstable and reached out to water which was
too shallow at low tide for many vessels. A massive programme of
reclamation and building undertaken by the fledgling Harbour Board,
formed in 1871, paved the way for the modern port. Now there is
industry and bulk oil storage and St Mary's Bay is a place of the past. City
vegetable and flower markets nestle close to the fishing basin where a
large fishing fleet offloads its catch in calm waters. To the east, beyond
the highrises of Queen Street, large reclamations yielded flat ground for
railway marshalling yards and new docks.

The Queen City developed in a haphazard and unplanned manner. The
North Shore was little more than a holiday resort served by vehicular
ferries until the Harbour Bridge linked it with the central city in 1959.
The proximity to the business area, sections with views of the harbour or
beach front access and later new industrial estates turned this into a
favoured area. But growth has come to the central city area, too, as the
multi-storeyed office blocks attest.

34

Sparkling waters. . .

YACHTS The 'sparkling waters' of the Waitemata are irresistible to Auckland boaties whether racing through the Rangitoto Channel as shown here or merely out for a Sunday afternoon family cruise. Year round the harbour is flecked with the white sails of yachts, and there is a vast choice of cruising grounds around the islands of the Gulf. Even on land, Aucklanders are always thinking nautically. Stickers on the back windows of their cars announce 'I'd rather be sailing'.

WESTHAVEN The wealthy and the not so wealthy rub fenders in the safe marinas of Westhaven beside the Harbour Bridge. The city's Waitemata Harbour offers many sheltered anchorages within its river estuaries and sandy bays, but more marinas are planned to cope with the growing number of boats. Thousands of Aucklanders own boats and many have built them themselves. Ferries and charter yachts, even an old restored steam tug, the William C. Daldy, ship others with salt in their blood into the sparkling waters.

Synonymous with Auckland are its never ending seascapes. Here, Bayswater and the Waitemata Harbour in the foreground, and two of the Hauraki Gulf's most famous islands further out. Low-lying Tiritiri-Matangi, known simply as Tiri by the locals, can be easily located at night by its exceptionally powerful light.

Beyond, Little Barrier rises majestically. The Maoris named it Hauturu — resting place of the wind — as the heights are frequently cloud-hidden. The whole island is a wildlife reserve and the virgin forests are a safe breeding ground for many rare and threatened species of bird and plant.

The natural advantages of the Waitemata Harbour and the northern proximity to world trade routes makes this New Zealand's busiest port. Over 6 million tonnes of varied cargo are shipped through Auckland and the smaller port of Onehunga on the Manukau Harbour, a short distance away on the other side of the isthmus. Highly mechanised and modern container facilities are serviced by motorway and rail depots radiating from the port.

The charm of many early Victorian buildings has been lost as modern high rise buildings and plazas have turned the colonial town into a contemporary city.

ALBERT PARK Stately palms and immense Morton Bay fig trees preside over Albert Park just two blocks from Queen Street bustle. The ornate clocktower of the adjacent university dating back to 1926 is an architectural link with the English academic tradition on which New Zealand's education system is based.

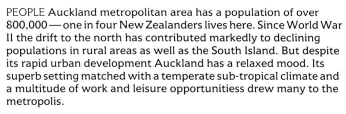

PEOPLE Auckland metropolitan area has a population of over 800,000 — one in four New Zealanders lives here. Since World War II the drift to the north has contributed markedly to declining populations in rural areas as well as the South Island. But despite its rapid urban development Auckland has a relaxed mood. Its superb setting matched with a temperate sub-tropical climate and a multitude of work and leisure opportunitiess drew many to the metropolis.

Some came from the Pacific Islands — Samoa, the Cooks, Tonga, Niue, Fiji, Tokelau — drawn by jobs and material advancement and immigration policies which reflect New Zealand's increasing awareness of her responsibilities to the South Pacific. In a few short years Auckland has become the world's largest Polynesian city. Inner city suburbs are brightened by hibiscus and gay flower patterned lavalavas. Boxes of taro sit on the footpath outside corner dairies. The British colonial town has become a multicultural, multilingual twentieth century city.

ONE TREE HILL A lone pine tree and an obelisk silhouette the One Tree Hill skyline. Its slopes, heavily scored by the trenches and terraces of the ancient pa, Mangakiekie, are testimony to many centuries of habitation and warfare.

WEST COAST Less than an hour's drive from downtown Auckland the indomitable raw energy of nature can be experienced on the moody West Coast and in the heavily bushed hills of the Waitakere Ranges inland.

Craggy misshapen cliffs and headlands are held apart by iron sand beaches and dunes, the black expanses constantly swept smooth by the prevailing onshore winds and the air misty with salt spray. This is an environment where people are dwarfed by the magnitude of the landscape.

Relics of an old bush railway at Karekare hark back to the days when the Waitakeres were a source of timber. Today the lush forests are protected reserves and water catchments criss-crossed by walking tracks.

Undeterred, indeed drawn by the elemental nature of the beaches, Aucklanders frequent the coast for recreation and food gathering. Year round surfers catch the big swells rolling in from the Tasman Sea while children are safe to play in the streams and lagoons. Rock fishermen risk dangerous conditions for good catches and at low tides mussels can be picked from the rocks.

PUKEKOHE An extensive view from Pukekohe Hill takes in a patchwork of fields, some grassed for dairying, others cultivated for the vegetable production for which the area is famed. The fertile volcanic loams here and at nearby Bombay, tilled by a mixed community of Chinese, Indian and Maori market gardeners, yield large crops of early onions and potatoes. With soils so productive that two or three crops can be grown annually, traditional vegetables are giving way to a new agriculture of export emphasis — kiwifruit and Nashi pears.

Settlers from Cornwall, Scotland and Ireland cleared the original puriri and kahikatea forests one hundred and forty years ago.

Their churches still bear signs of stockading and scars from battles with Maoris alerted to the value of the land. At Tuakau, on a bluff high above the Waikato River, the well preserved Alexandra Redoubt is another historic remnant of the bloody Waikato Campaigns of 1863-65. During these years the Waikato tribes valiantly resisted the British forces and their defeat saw their lands transferred to military settlers.

Each January Pukekohe is abuzz with excitement as New Zealand's International Grand Prix is contested on the Pukekohe Raceway. The whine of high performance formula cars and smell of high octane fuel encroach on the peaceable countryside.

Export industries...

RACE HORSES Waikato stud farms, like this one near Cambridge, breed some of the land's finest racehorses. Over the years carefully selected bloodstock from England, Ireland and America has been brought here to steadily improve the pedigrees and has resulted in a thriving export industry.

HUNTLY On the fringe of the Waikato dairylands and at the centre of New Zealand's largest coalfield is the massive Huntly Power Station. When fully commissioned at the end of 1985, its four steam-driven turbines will produce 1000 Megawatts of electricity, 50% more than the eight hydro-electric stations already along the Waikato River.

KINLEITH Forestry constitutes one of New Zealand's major industries and forest products are the country's fourth largest export group. Over half of the exotic forests are in the central North Island on the volcanic plateau. There the dark green pines march across the landscape in one orderly row after another and huge trucks, top-heavy with logs, thunder towards timber, pulp and paper mills or the overseas ships at the Port of Tauranga. In the mid-1950s the two main timber companies built huge processing plants at Kawerau and Tokoroa. These company towns boomed and Tokoroa's Kinleith Mill, pictured here, employs 4,000 people in its production of clean timber, kraft pulp and paper.

COROMANDEL Emergent ratas tower above the canopy of the Coromandel bush.

The northern rata reaches its greatness only at the expense of some other tree. In an intimate form of cannibalism the seeds of the rata lodge themselves in a cranny on another tree and develop into an epiphyte. This in turn sends roots down to the forest floor and begins to grow around the host tree, embracing it so tightly that it eventually dies. In time the rata stems fuse forming a large hollow trunk, supporter of the mass of leaves and branches perhaps 30 metres overhead.

MARTHA MINE PUMPHOUSE The Martha Mine at Waihi became, in its seventy years of operation, one of the wealthiest gold mines in the world. A maze of shafts and tunnels pursued the quartz veins directly beneath the town's streets. In 60 years they yielded $360 million of gold and silver. The concrete ruins of the Number 5 Pumphouse pictured here along with huge cyanide storage tanks nearby are all that is left of this famous mine.

FOUR SQUARE STORE This old store dates from the turn of the century at the time Waihi's Martha mine was producing over £1 million of bullion a year. When the mine closed in 1952 the township quietly continued as a service centre to the surrounding farmland. The many old buildings and the Waihi Museum keep alive the link with the past.

Alternative living. . .

COROMANDEL Beyond the tranquil farmlands that fringe the harbours and riverheads at Coromandel, Colville, Whitianga and Tairua, rise the steep, craggy backbone of the Coromandel Ranges.

Along their length, within the 65,000 hectares of the Coromandel Forest Park, Northland-type rainforests blend with southern species. Within the dense bush too, rarities like the native frog (Leiopelma archeyi — a tiny creature which cannot croak, only squeak, whose huge eyes bulge like an alligator's and whose young are born straight from the egg skipping the tadpole stage), massive kauris like Tane Nui (47m high, 10m girth), and rumours of monsters (the Moehau Monster) have survived rapacious quests for timber and gold.

ALTERNATIVE LIVING At the end of a narrow potholed track running into the hills behind Waikawau Bay is the community of Karuna Falls, one of a number of communes at the isolated northern tip of the Coromandel. Influenced by the social revolution of the 1960s, many young New Zealanders returned to the land. Rejecting the nuclear family and the importance of material wealth, many saw the land as a clue in the search for an alternative lifestyle. In a manner not too dissimilar to the communal ownership and extended family of the traditional Maori system, groups of people pooled funds and resources. On blocks of scrubby undeveloped but cheap land the social experiments commenced. Some had complete self-sufficiency as a goal. Others blended modern farming techniques with communal attitudes. All felt they must respect their environment and many regarded their land as sanctuaries for regenerating bush. The Coromandel is a haven for alternative living and the energy of these new settlers has done much to revitalise a declining area.

BUFFALO BEACH In summer the safe waters and white sands of Whitianga's Buffalo Beach are crowded with holiday makers. They are attracted to the beautiful beaches, the superb fishing and diving, the boating among the myriad of offshore islands. Inland they scour the streams for semi-precious stones. In winter the town is deserted and the easterly gales that keep the fishing fleet tied up at the wharf are no different from those that drove H.M.S. Buffalo aground here in 1840.

Captain James Cook observed the transit of the planet Mercury here in 1769 during his first circumnavigation of New Zealand. He named Mercury Bay to commemorate the event and his landing place, a long beach to the east of Whitianga, is Cook's Beach.

MILL CREEK, TAIRUA These fertile river plains at Tairua are among the few flatlands on the Coromandel Peninsula. Elsewhere tendrils of farmland reach into the scrub from the easier land bordering the harbours and rivers. For the most part the brooding hills of the Coromandel Ranges are covered in dense rainforest.

KIWIFRUIT These carefully laid out vines will produce kiwifruit, a furry brown fruit with tasty green flesh that has been responsible for a spectacular export boom. Thousands of trays of this subtropical fruit are air and sea freighted each year to Europe, Japan and North America to be sold as a gourmet delight.

CORN Corn sprouts up around this old Maori whare (house). By the time it reaches maturity only the roof will be visible. In years gone by the Maoris seized on the new European crops, and using their age-old horticultural skills and their own boats to transport the produce to Auckland, and even across the Tasman, they had a busy trade established during the mid-nineteenth century.

Now, maize land and dairying country throughout the Bay of Plenty are being displaced by horticulture, in particular kiwifruit and avocados.

WHITE ISLAND 50 kilometres offshore from Whakatane in the expansive Bay of Plenty, one of New Zealand's most spectacular landmarks announces its presence with billowing clouds of steam and ash. This is the intensely active volcano, White Island, where thermal activity has enlarged the crater and dropped it below sea level. Poisonous gases belch out constantly and in 1977 an andesite lava eruption occurred. No wonder then that attempts to mine sulphur here in the early days were short-lived.

WHAKATANE Overlooking the prosperous town of Whakatane, central to the long crescent of the Bay of Plenty, is an ancient pa site. Reputedly built by Toi, one of the earliest Polynesian explorers to reach these shores, it is an historical reminder that much of the country's early settlement occurred here. The famous Arawa canoe landed at Maketu a bit further up the coast and the Mataatua made landfall at the Whakatane River heads.

HOUSE Flowers and beautiful gardens are inevitable where a warm sun shines for a higher than average 2200 hours a year. Keen gardeners have made the Bay of Plenty area full of horticultural delights. Near Whakatane the Indian Gardens reproduce an oriental setting and at Awakeri orchids are grown commercially. Botanical displays blend with aviaries at Katikati's Bird Gardens and Tauranga's elegant public gardens are worth visiting.

MATATA MAIZE The climate of the Bay of Plenty and the arable coastlands is ideal for growing maize and during the 1970s production boomed as many farmers made a shift to mixed farming. This orderly crop at Matata will probably become supplementary feed for dairy cows on the neighbouring Rangitaiki Plains.

WHITIANGA Informal campsites such as this one at Whitianga Bay, north of Opotiki are permitted on this coast unspoiled by commercial development. Pohutukawa line the seaside and for a few weeks early in summer.

KOHI POINT On the hills between Whakatane and its resort neighbour, Ohope, a sheep farmer keeps an eye on his flock with the help of his well-trained work mates, the highly valued sheep dogs. Sheep farming, and fat-lamb production especially, occupies the low coastal hill areas and supplements the rich dairying region of the plains.

Action rivers. . .

RANGITAIKI AND WAIOEKA RIVER SPORTS Since earliest times rivers have provided natural communication and travel routes. In New Zealand a combination of canoe and portage trails laced the North Island allowing Maori and early European travellers far-ranging destinations. But it was not until twentieth century technology was adroitly applied by a New Zealand farmer that the hindrances of shallow rapids and fast flowing narrows were overcome.

A farmer in the Mackenzie country saw that the obvious 'roads' into the mountains were the rivers. In 1954 Mr C.W.F. Hamilton produced the first jet engine suitable for use on a shallow-drafted boat.

The jet boat is now used world wide. In its country of origin it has become indispensible to farmers, hunters and tourists. Pictured here speeding up the Bay of Plenty's Rangitaiki River is a 10-seater craft which takes sightseers on a 1½ hour trip. The thrilling ride contrasts narrow gorges with stretches of calm, willow lined open waters and culminates in an exciting climb up whitewater rapids to the foot of the Aniwhenua Falls.

To white water rafting, there are no boundaries beyond the direction of flow. This sport which relishes waterfalls, rapids and whirlpools has taken New Zealand by storm. Literally at times. Up and down the country waterways have been graded by the New Zealand Rafting Association and are filled every weekend by keen rafters.

PORT OHOPE The small harbour of Ohiwa and the much larger one at Tauranga are the only indentations in the otherwise continuous arc of coastline from Cape Runaway to the Coromandel Peninsula.

At Wainui, opposite the slender arm of the Ohiwa Peninsula, the infamous but much celebrated guerilla fighter of the last century's Land Wars, Te Kooti, spent his last years after being granted pardon. His final resting place remains a secret.

58

Own brand of cowboy. . .

CATTLE DROVER, OPAPE Along the beaches, roads and by special droving routes across the hills, cattle are taken to new pastures by this country's own brand of cowboy. No motorbikes for these men who show off their riding skills in the rings of the Cape's rodeo carnival.

For decades droving has been a practical way to move large numbers of stock around Poverty Bay and the East Cape. The sheep and cattle stations here also supply replacement stock for farms as far distant as the Waikato but the big long-distance drives are becoming fewer with the passing years.

MOTU The Motu (meaning isolated place) River has its source high in the steep terrain of the Raukumara Ranges, the bush-clad greywacke hills which bisect the East Cape from north-east to south-west.

Trout are fished from its tributaries and where the river meets the sea, surf casters line up.

This coastline is one of the most beautiful the North Island has to offer and the 340 km of provincial highway from Opotiki to Gisborne offers magic scenery and contact with a stronghold of Maoridom. Over half of the population is Maori and the carved meeting houses of maraes scatter the route.

Few roads pierce the interior. The Motu Road, following old Maori tracks, here opens up a backcountry valley at Toatoa.

LOTTIN POINT From Opotiki to Te Kaha dairying is possible on limited coastal flats and on the opposite coast is restricted to pockets of alluvial plains such as those around Ruatoria. Elsewhere sheep and cattle are grazed and on these slopes at Lottin Point a farm climbs up from the sea.

Finest carvers. . .

EAST CAPE High on the bluffs of East Cape an isolated lighthouse guards treacherous waters where storms arise without warning.

Above the Cape the legendary Mt Hikurangi, the Sky Peak, symbol of unity for the Ngati Porou, catches the first sunrays of dawn.

Close by Te Araroa boasts not only the country's easternmost hotel but a massive pohutukawa, the largest of them all and thought to be over 600 years old, with 22 trunks and a spread of 37 metres.

TIKITIKI CHURCH Skilfully carved and highly decorated Maori churches feature largely around the East Coast, a region which has produced some of the finest carvers and extant carvings. St Mary's Church at Tikitiki, probably the most ornate anywhere, is dedicated to Ngati Porou servicemen of WWI. Two of these men are pictured in the east window. The patterns on the rafters (kowhaiwhai) and the carved panels (poupou) record Ngati Porou history.

TE PUIA Only in the last few years has the tarseal replaced the gravel on the shingle road that meanders around the East Cape. All along the way, sienna red woolstores, like this one near Te Puia, line the route.

Sheepfarming is the mainstay occupation in these parts. But unlike neighbouring Hawke Bay, this is not a wealthy region, although the East Coast's isolation from the mainstream of twentieth century New Zealand has ensured an unhurried and peaceful approach to life. Moreover, with a high proportion of the land remaining in Maori ownership and with the majority of the population Maori, this is a unique area where the ways of Maoridom are alive and well.

SHEEP MUSTER A sheep muster on the Tatapouri Hills near Gisborne, with cabbage trees prominent on the hillsides. This plant is not a tree at all, but is actually related to the New Zealand flaxes. Its name probably comes from the flavour of the edible inner leaves.

The extensive sheep stations with their flocks of wool-producing Romneys dominate East Cape farming. They are the result of extensive land clearing, begun after 1870, once conflicts fired by Te Kooti's determination to revenge his imprisonment and confiscation of his people's land had ended.

ERODED HILLS The zealousness of the first European sheep farmers during the late nineteenth and early twentieth centuries to clear the then forested ranges of Hawke Bay and East Cape has left a bare countryside prone to erosion.

Pockets of exotic pine forest have been planted not only for timber but for vital erosion control.

TOKOMARU BAY The migratory canoe, Tokomaru, is namesake of this small farming and resort area on the East Coast although the local Ngati Porou are descended from the Takitimu and Horouta canoes. Long an area of Maori habitation — there is a historic pa on Te Mawhai Point, to the south end of the beach — this was also one of Captain James Cook's first regions of contact.

While the *Endeavour* anchored at neighbouring Anaura Bay for provisioning, the botanists, Banks and Solander, made the first European observations of New Zealand's flora and fauna. They found the country to be 'agreeable beyond description . . . a kind of second Paradise'.

In time whalers made East Cape a centre of their operations and one of the largest whaling stations was here at Tokomaru. Remains of an old freezing works bears witness to the abandonment of the sea highway once the road was eased along the coast.

RURAL PATCHWORK Aerial views of the diverse crop fields of the Waipaoa River Valley reveal a delightful chequerwork. This small but bountiful plain with Gisborne on its seaward boundary, produces vegetables such as beans, tomatoes and asparagus, for a large processing plant in the town.

KUMARA Kumara (*Ipomoea batatas*) is a golden-fleshed sweet potato that is a favourite vegetable on New Zealand tables. It is equally delicious roasted, English style, or steamed in a Maori hangi.

The kumara is native to South America and how this tuber reached the islands of Polynesia remains the subject of anthropological research and conjecture. It is clear though that the second phase of immigrants to this country — explained in Maori mythology as a great fleet of ocean-going canoes sailing down from Polynesia — brought the kumara with them.

KUMARA The cultivation of this vegetable changed the early patterns of living dramatically. Whereas the early moahunters had led a nomadic existence following the large flightless, emu-like birds that were easy prey, the Maori population now concentrated in warmer regions of the North Island where the new tropical plants — kumara, and to a lesser extent taro and gourd — could be grown. Permanent villages were built near the growing grounds in an intricate system of warfare, the other main feature of this 'classic Maori' period, that may well have been stimulated in the first instance by disputes over good land.

Happily today, a purchase at the greengrocer's is all that is needed to acquire the kumara for dinner.

Roadside stalls like these near Bay of Plenty's Matata give kids a chance to earn some pocket money. Fresh bargains and honesty-box stalls are bonuses of rural living.

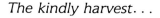

MAHIA PENINSULA The long sandy beaches, the tiny sheltered port of Waikokopu, historical pa sites and dramatic scenery all surrounded by sea plentiful with fish, shellfish and crayfish contribute to make the Mahia Peninsula a delightful boundary between Hawke Bay and Poverty Bay.

Repeating age old gathering instincts, members of the Mahia Fishing Co-op gather their harvest from a traditional food area. Some can probably trace their lineage back to Whatonga, one of the early Pacific navigators to settle in this land. An abundance of food and the hot pools a short distance away at Morere have made this a favoured dwelling place for many centuries. The first Europeans here were whalers in the mid-1800s. For twenty years trypots at eight stations on the Peninsula boiled down blubber from the unfortunate prey. Now farmers, fishermen and holidaymakers make up the population.

NAPIER Napier's Bluff Hill offers a panoramic view across the city (population 50,800) to the southern sweep of the fish-hook shaped Hawke Bay. Beyond are the luxuriant Heretaunga Plains where three rivers meander down to the Bay and Napier's sister city, Hastings, earns a reputation as 'Fruit Bowl of New Zealand'.

ORMOND VALLEY As New Zealanders increasingly develop a taste for wine, the local grape industry burgeons. From vineyards in the three main growing areas at Blenheim, Henderson (West Auckland) and Gisborne/ Hastings come award winning vintages. Here in the Ormond Valley near Gisborne, Reisling, Sylvaner and Palamino vines respond to a mild climate with plentiful sunshine particularly suited to white table wine production.

TARAWERA A phantom war canoe seen on Lake Tarawera was interpreted by a 110 year old tohunga as a warning of disaster. Eleven days later, in June 1886, the supposedly extinct Mt Tarawera blew itself apart in an explosion heard as far away as Christchurch, and rent open a 20 km split clearly visible across the mountain.
Ash and pumice showered an area of 16,000 square kilometres, completely covering three nearby settlements and killing many people. The 'Buried Village' of Te Wairoa was perfectly preserved and is gradually being excavated from under 3 metres of mud and ash. The village used to be the departure point for visits to the world-famous pink and white terraces, also destroyed in the eruption.

CRATERS OF THE MOON Between the active volcanoes at Tongariro National Park and the steaming White Island a major fault line slashes across the North Island, creating a region of unique and spectacular thermal activity. This is one of only three places in the world (the others are Iceland and Yellowstone Park) where hot water and steam vent in sky-reaching geysers.

Boiling, bubbling mud and hot springs are further manifestations of the earth's raw energy. Bores at Taupo and Rotorua draw steam for domestic heating and mineral baths, and at Wairakei the geothermal power station pioneers specialised technology for electricity generation.

MOKAI VILLAGE In the hinterland of Lake Taupo's northern shores abandoned mill towns like Mokai are gently slipping back into the shadows of time. Gone is the bustle of the mill, the bush railway, the company store. Gone too are the stands of native bush that were the lifeblood of the village. Visitors are few and many of those that do make their way along the pumice tracks are artists and photographers enticed by the picturesque decline and decay.

Thermal spectacular. . .

SILICA POOLS Silica, dissolved underground by the hot waters of the chloride springs, is deposited on the surface as the water cools. At Whakarewarewa, the famous thermal reserve in the heart of Rotorua city, several acres of silica terraces and pools are interspersed with geysers and mud pools. The most majestic of the geysers, Pohutu, sometimes plays for hours up to a height of 30 metres.

LAKE OKATAINA The tranquility of unspoilt native bush, exotic with tree ferns and native fuchsia, and tiny white beaches edging clear trout-packed waters render Lake Okataina one of the finest jewels in the necklace of lakes surrounding Rotorua.

BUSH STUMPS On land cleared hastily of bush, rotting tree stumps are all that remain of the former forest. In the aftermath of World War II country around Rotorua was provided to ex-servicemen for sheep farming. While pockets of this difficult pumice land have been put to agricultural use, forestry is now providing a more successful land use. Exotic introductions to the landscape: pine trees and power pylons.

TIMBER Timber! New Zealand's history and development since the arrival of Europeans has been inextricably linked to its forests. The first exports were kauri spars for the navvies of Europe; later timber was shipped to the growing colony of Australia. Large tracts of the seemingly endless 'bush' were burnt off to clear farmland, and sheep and cattle, with the advent of refrigerated ships, became the country's new export 'crop'. Meanwhile, the needs of an expanding local population had to be met and in the hills trees continued to be felled.

By the turn of the century, planners realised that if the milling of the indigenous forests proceeded at the same rate, the hitherto great forests would be exhausted by the 1940s. Today the traveller finds mile after mile of orderly, man planted forests in the central North Island. They are spectacular evidence of the reaction to that early warning. The use of imported softwood species, mainly Pinus radiata, has helped reverse the trend to depletion and over twenty percent of New Zealand's land area still remains in indigenous forest.

Gone are the canvas bush towns and the crosscut saw pits. The modern timber worker lives in orderly mill towns and does his job with chainsaws, huge caterpillar tractors and powerful logging trucks.

Yet at Agricultural Shows and Field Days competitions founded on the skills of the early axemen and sawyers hold their popularity.

'Axemen! Stand to your Logs!' The cry of the starter rings out and grips tighten on axes which have been carefully sharpened and stored in their special carrying boxes until the competition. It's the standing block event and the spectators watch closely, noting the axeman's stance, how clean a cut he makes and how well he avoids a hard knot in his block.

This is a man's world. The physique of the competitors reflects long hours of tough physical work 'down in the bush' — as well as keen appetites and a thirst for beer! Many of these men are following the traditions of their bushmen fathers and grandfathers.

Chainsaws have crept into the competitions on the circuit of late — much to the displeasure of the old timers. But the classic events are still firmly grounded in early timber methods. Take the tree-felling, or jigger-cut, contest. When the early bushmen had to fight their way through the dense Antipodean undergrowth, it was to hell with the English method of cutting close to the ground. Throw up a few jigger boards and climb above it, mate!

The crosscut sawyers sweat their way through their log. Many make their own saws which can measure 3.5 metres long.

The public arena is a chance to show off skills that are often hidden deep down the end of a logging track in the comparative solitude of the bush.

Elsewhere at the show other contests based on rural livelihoods are being held. They range from dog trials to spinning competitions. And with a New Zealand horseman taking a gold medal for the first time in an Equestrian event at the 1984 Olympics, the show jumpers are inspired.

Fisherman's delight. . .

LAKE TAUPO Taupo township faces south across New Zealand's largest lake, an inland sea of 616 square kilometres, towards the grandeur of the Tongariro National Park mountains.

At the geographical centre of the North Island this pleasant city is a popular holiday spot. The Lake itself offers fishing, sailing, charter cruises, water-skiing and swimming and sightseeing float planes use its waters as an airstrip. Tranquil enough in the height of summer, winter storms can transform these waters into dangerous and uninviting seas.

The lake has formed in a 'caldera', a huge crater left by an eruption of immense magnitude 2000 years ago. A rhyolitic explosion of the same type as Tarawera, it spewed out pumice over a vast area reaching northwards almost to Auckland.

TROUT FISHING Lake Taupo and its tributary rivers are a trout fisherman's delight for both fly casting and trolling. The pink-banded rainbow and the brown trout have flourished here since their introduction late last century from California and Tasmania and fish weighing up to 3.5kg frequently reward patient anglers.

TAUPO A tranquil scene as the sun drops low in the western sky, silhouetting a family catching the last moments of a day on one of Lake Taupo's numerous beaches. At times like this, the grandness of the landscape can overwhelm a person and a sense of isolation and smallness is not misplaced.

Restless land. . .

MT RUAPEHU Beyond old wild roses, above Taupo's rolling hills and the tussock of the Rangipo Desert, rises the snowcap of the North Island's highest peak, Mt Ruapehu. This mountain, and its sacred neighbours, Tongariro and Ngauruhoe, were gifted to the nation by the Ngati Tuwharetoa in 1887 to become the basis for the Tongariro National Park.

Undeterred by the volatility of these geologically young andesite mountains, which have all erupted within living memory, trampers, climbers and skiers swarm the slopes of this popular all-season resort.

WAITETOKO CHURCH From 1839 missionary-explorers began to bring their Christian message to the Tuwharetoa people of the Taupo area, challenging beliefs which went back to Rangi (the sky god) and Papa (the earth mother), the principles of tapu (sacred) and noa (free from tapu) and the role of the tohunga (priest). For those Maoris who believed in the supreme being, Io, the new religion was readily assimilated.

However, by the time the missionaries reached the shores of Taupo there was some scepticism that they might be land dealers. And confusion arose from the bickering between the various denominations. The choice on one occasion was made by putting two missionaries to a trial by ordeal. Who could sit on hot coals (sans pants) for the longest? One declined, the other won a new parish by default. One wonders if this picturesque church at Waitetoko has a tale or two of its own?

RAETIHI Ratana temples like this one near Raetihi are devoid of traditional Maori art and are quite different from other Christian churches. They are charged with symbolism. The twin towers, typical of Ratana churches, stand for the Saints Arepa and Omeka, the alpha and the omega, the beginning and the end.

WANGANUI RIVER From headwaters high on the slopes of Mt Ruapehu and from the rugged wilderness of the King Country the Wanganui River wends its way through a landscape alive with history and luxuriant with natural beauty to meet the Tasman Sea.

RATANA The orderly Rangitikei township of Ratana, population 400, owes its origin to a religious experience. In 1918 Tuhupotiki Rata had a vision of an angel. Throwing aside his drinking and betting, this champion ploughman and horseman began to preach the virtues of Jehovah and urged the end of the old Maori superstitions. His successes with faith healing brought converts flocking to the district, and he founded the Ratana church which currently has a following of 35,000 strong.

Maori myth. . .

MAUI FIELD Taranaki's role as an energy supplier was first hinted at as early as 1856 when oil was found in a suburb of the region's main town, New Plymouth. The small well produced 'Peak' petrol until 1972.

Driven by rocketing oil prices and subsequently the desire for self-sufficiency in fuel, the government backed extensive exploration programmes. In 1962 natural gas was discovered at Kapuni and just seven years later the vast Maui gasfield was detected offshore. Its location far beneath a seabed of exposed ocean 40 kilometres from land meant the importation of massive production platforms, like the one pictured here, and North Sea technology.

PARIOKARIWA POINT Hedges offer shelter on Taranaki's windswept coast. The soils here are heavily weathered by the prevailing westerlies and the high rainfall. Heavy dressings of superphosphate and potash along with progressive use of new grasses and high stocking increase the fertility of the land and boost farm production.

WAVERLY When Mt Egmont's graceful slopes are enshrouded in mist the mountain is said to be weeping for his love, Pihanga. In one of the great Maori myths is found the explanation for Taranaki's solitary position. In the time before men the North Island mountains lived together on the central plateau. The only female was the beautiful Pihanga. Feuding with the weapons of eruption, smoke and fire, the mountains fought for her love. Tongariro was the victor. Reluctantly Taranaki retreated westwards, his path marked by the gouge of the Wanganui River Valley. Thus this sad mountain rests in mournful isolation. Taranaki, the Maori name, means 'barren mountain' and is perhaps more appropriate than Captain Cook's commemoration of the First Lord of the Admiralty.

SOUTH TARANAKI For twenty-five kilometres in all directions, the mantle of pasturelands gullied by countless streams radiates out from Mt Egmont. The wealth of this small but densely populated province relies heavily on the prosperous dairy farms which vie with those of the Waikato for top production.

Sands of time. . .

TONGAPORUTU For centuries the Tasman Sea has gnawed away the Tongaporutu cliffs, sculpting caverns and tunnels in the sandstone. Ancient Maori rock drawings have been found in one of the large caves. This area, traditional boundary between the Taranaki and Waikato tribes, was the scene of territorial conflicts in pre-European times. However, faced with armed British militia confiscating their land during the 1860s, long-standing enemies joined forces to resist the new invaders.

AOTEA HARBOUR Shoals and sandbars, shellfish and schnapper. And not many people. The same description could apply to all the harbours which penetrate the North Island's West Coast. Aotea Harbour, flanked by Raglan and Kawhia, is no exception. Splendid in its isolation, visited by hardy travellers via twisting gravel roads, and known well only by the locals who live on its shores and farm the boundaries, the Aotea is one of those places the world has passed by. The sands of Ruapuke Beach between Aotea Harbour and distant Karioi Mountain hide one of New Zealand's mysteries: the remains of an old boat of unknown origin. On a rare occasion when nature swept the sands aside a century ago, observers noted teak diagonal planking fastened with wooden trenails and brass bolts and a bronze plate inscribed with strange characters which bore a resemblance to those on the Tamil Bell, another subject of conjecture. A ship's bell of probably Indian origin, it was discovered by the missionary, Colenso, in Whangarei, in 1836, being used as a cooking pot. How did it get there? Who brought it? No one has yet provided the answers.

83

Pioneering days. . .

HISTORIC VILLAGE With its verandah sheltering the front door, and the leanto out the back, the simple worker's cottage of the English countryside was altered by the immigrants to become New Zealand's unique settler's house. This fine example near Palmerston North dates back to the Manawatu's early organised immigrant settlements such as that of Feilding in the 1870s.

BARN & WHEATFIELD, MARTON The alluvial plains of Marton, protected from marauding coastal sands by forest reclamations, are well watered, and highly productive. Here the wheatfields evoke images of the grain-growing belt of America.

PAPAWAI The Papawai marae at Greytown in the Wairarapa Valley, currently under restoration, was known as the Maori Capital during the 1890s. The Kotahitanga, the Maori Parliament, was convened here in an attempt to establish total self-government for the Maori. As it had superceded the Maori King Movement, so its ideas were in turn absorbed and amended by the Young Maori Party whose statesmen (Sir Apirana Ngata, Sir Peter Buck, Sir Maui Pomare) worked through the national Parliament and achieved much for the welfare of their Maori people.

ARAMOANA Stately mansions such as Aramoana on the Wairarapa coast hark back to the large sheep stations of last century. The grace of homesteads like this belies the difficulties of the pioneering days. Until 1928 Aramoana's link with the outside was by coastal packet alone.

While the extensive holdings have today been divided into smaller units, many of the coast's farming families can trace their links to the original pioneers.

No Refuge. . .

WAIMARAMA South of Waimarama the coastal hills lie wrinkled beneath green pastures and browsing sheep. Rapid erosion demolishes mudstone and papa soils. Bluffs and promontories follow one after the other save for a few wild beaches.

NGAWIHI The Aorangi Mountains drop steeply into the sea at Cape Palliser, granting no snug harbours or easy fishing grounds. The crayfishers at Ngawihi must haul their boats out after each sortie. Crayfish, or lobster as it is called by diners in America and Europe, is easy to eat but difficult and risky to catch from small boats rising and falling on Pacific swells in reef strewn waters.

SHIPWRECK Two hundred and fifty ungiving kilometres of Wairarapa coast separate the ports of Napier and Wellington. For ships running before a storm there is no refuge on this rocky shore where sandstone reefs can wait treacherously several kilometres out to sea.
This rusting hull at Honeycomb Rock is a recent victim and is one of many that scatter the foreshore.

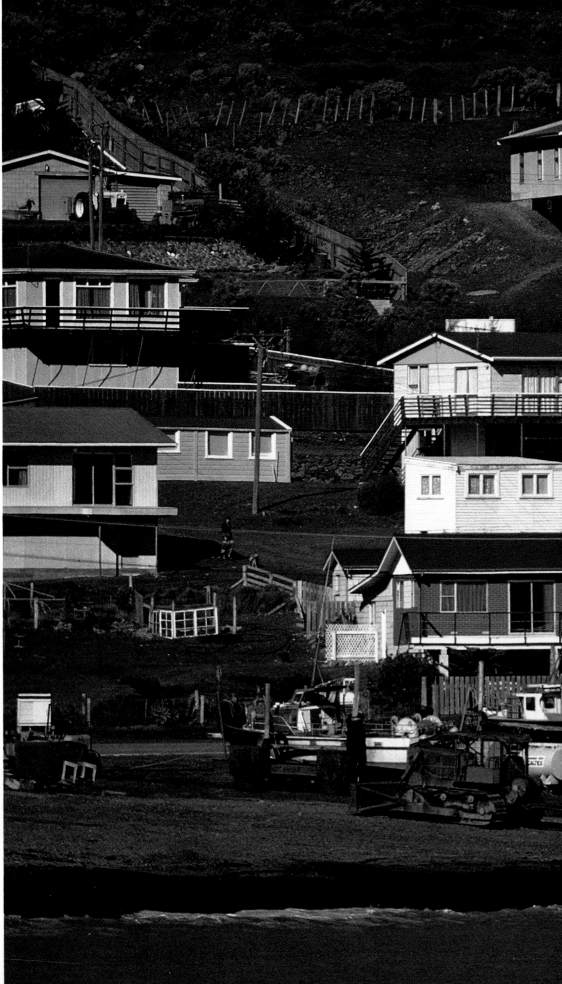

The 'Gold Coast'...

PARAPARAUMU At day's end, the sun setting behind the distant South Island projects a warm glow along the beaches of the 'Gold Coast'. Here at Paraparaumu, Raumati, Paekakariki, and Waikanae, Wellingtonians find weekend relaxation on the expansive surf beaches and enjoy temperatures which are always a few degrees warmer than at home.

LOOKING NORTH Wellington clings to steep faulted greywacke hills on the south-western shores of a splendid natural harbour.

Motorway and railway follow the Wellington Fault south along the only land route in to the capital city.

In the far distance are the plains of the Hutt River Valley backed by the Rimutaka Ranges. Intensive industrial development in the twin cities of Upper and Lower Hutt balances the primarily administrative role of the capital.

WELLINGTON Sweeping into the heart of downtown Wellington, the motorway funnels more vehicles into an already congested space. Many of the personable aspects of the old city have been lost or disrupted by motorway planning lacking a wider vision of the human environment.

ORIENTAL BAY At Oriental Bay on the slopes of Mt Victoria, inner city living combines with the pleasures of a beach resort. Facing north to catch the sun all day, this is a favoured residential area, moments from the central city.

MIRIMAR PENINSULA Where Maori pas once defended Te Whanganui-a-Tara, the great harbour of Tara, Mirimar's sprawling suburbs and parklands (and a prison) now watch over the narrow Wellington harbour entrance. (Left of picture.)

ORIENTAL PARADE Above Oriental Parade a medley of terraced houses crowds the hill-side.

WELLINGTON The hub of Wellington; the hub of the nation. Emanating from the distinctive 'Beehive' and the surrounding buildings of government come the directives for New Zealand's 3.1 million people.

A stone's throw away rail and sea transports link to close the distance between the North and South Islands.

The Railway Station is also the terminus for crowded electric commuter trains which daily disgorge hundreds of white-collar workers from dormitory suburbs along the Hutt Valley and around the Porirua Basin behind the western hills.

SEDDON STATUE In front of the pillared, Takaka marble, Parliament Buildings of New Zealand's House of Representatives, the statue of the country's second Liberal Prime Minister, Richard John Seddon (P.M. 1893-1906) looks out over the fore-court where pigeons, protests and pageantry are all to be found at one time or another in a typical year.

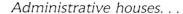

MALL One of the delights of Wellington is its varied architecture and the malls of the downtown area are no exception.

The streets are narrow, byways are steep paths and steps. The city crowds in on itself, forced by the nature of its site into an intimacy and cosmopolitanism which sets Wellington apart from the other main cities of New Zealand.

HOUSE Innovative modern design blends with pockets of Victorian wooden cottages to give Wellington a unique architecture. And the people who live in these homes see themselves as a brand apart from other Antipodeans, united through having braved the steep hills and boisterous climate.

WELLINGTON RUNNERS In Wellington as in Auckland the waterfront is level training ground for runners. Land reclamations since the 1850s have slowly but surely extended the business district to today's size. The scarcity of sites has made the real estate here some of the most expensive in New Zealand. Recent rebuilding to comply with new earthquake requirements has given the city centre a new architectural image, as the glass-fronted high rises and shopping malls displace the older buildings of a colonial past.

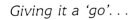

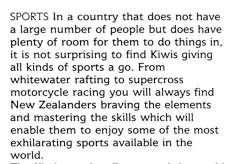

SPORTS In a country that does not have a large number of people but does have plenty of room for them to do things in, it is not surprising to find Kiwis giving all kinds of sports a go. From whitewater rafting to supercross motorcycle racing you will always find New Zealanders braving the elements and mastering the skills which will enable them to enjoy some of the most exhilarating sports available in the world.

The Kiwis continually astound the world by producing Olympic-class surfsailers, canoeists and yachtsmen from a population that would not fill many of the world's cities. There has been a new emphasis on sport that has come with each success and with the popularisation of new sports by live TV coverage. Rugby, soccer, hockey, cricket and basketball are more popular now than ever and the annual Round the Bays run has developed almost a cult following — yet away from the crowds you will still find people enjoying some of the world's greenest golf courses and best deep-sea fishing in a country that provides it all.

South Island Introduction . . .

If the North Island is coloured by regional diversity, in both its inhabitants and landscape, the South Island is marked by contrasts of a more extreme nature. Soaring mountains border level plains. West Coast rainforests contrast with the arid Central Otago farmlands. These contrasts result from the workings of the South Island's primary elements — earth and water.

Nevertheless, the 'mainlanders', as they call themselves, reflect regional differences too. The 'Coasters' are an independent lot, many with Irish goldminers in their family histories. The high country breeds self-sufficient solitary types, and there is a propriety associated with people from Canterbury and Otago. In Southland New Zealanders' only true regional accent is found.

From the north-east to the south-west, the prima donnas of the south, lofty and elegant in costumes of pristine snow, parade their way down the length of the island. The Southern Alps are at once imposing, occasionally serene in silhouette against azure skies, and often brooding beneath cloaks of storm clouds hiding their slopes. Disguised thus, these barriers to the westerly weather ensure the longevity of New Zealand's traditional name, Aotearoa.

It's an impressive range, comparable to the Alps of Europe, and is the backbone and *raison d'etre* of this landmass. Millions of years ago, during geological eras of a time scale beyond ready understanding, the earth's crust crumpled, rising up over itself along a marked fault line, convulsing with the tumult of mountain building. Ancient rocks surfaced. Others were transformed by overwhelming pressures.

In the process substances that would later prove valuable were created — in particular, coal and gold. The latter would, during the 1860s, draw prospectors from all over the world to Central Otago and Westland and lay the foundations for South Island prosperity for many years.

However, it was pounamu — greenstone — that was the most precious of stones to the Maori. In keeping with age-old traditions occurring in many cultures, jade provided the perfect material for weapons, ornaments and tools. As it only occurs in six locations in the South Island, and as metal was not known to the Maoris, the value placed on greenstone was enormous. From the highland region of Lake Wakatipu came inanga, a pearly grey-green variety, painstakingly shaped into the prized, deadly weapon, the patu ponamu. Other locations in the Sounds and up the rivers of the West Coast demanded arduous journeys of recovery. The southern tribes, whose small numbers were familiar with the mountain passes, traded extensively with those of the north in exchange for kumara. Elaborate patterns of trade and gift giving spread the prized ponamu throughout the land.

The final shaping of the land profile was, in the North Island, dominated by volcanic eruptions. But in the South Island the dominant force was the glaciers. The low temperatures of successive ice ages weighted the Alps with unbearable loads of compacted snow and frozen water. Solid ice ground a path between the peaks, clawing its way down the slopes, carving out huge high-walled valleys, and dragging tonnes of rocky debris from the mountains. The glaciers flowed, retreated and grew again, each time dumping moraine in their path. And from their terminal faces, rivers carried the gravel downstream to form the vast plains of Southland and Canterbury.

Glaciers still flow from the Southern Alps, fed by the snow fields of Mt Aspiring, Mt Cook and Mt Tasman. On the eastern side of the divide several flow through Mt Cook National Park, where the chance to ski the Tasman Glacier is an added attraction in a region, naturally enough, already renowned for its alpine-sports opportunities.

On the opposite side of the range, the Franz Joseph and Fox Glaciers survive an astounding journey from freezing altitudes to the temperate coast. It is contrasts such as this — rainforest and fern backgrounded by glaciers and mountain — that intrigue tourists and earn the South Island its special reputation amongst travellers. There are few countries where scenery and mood alter so dramatically, so quickly.

Flora and fauna also exhibit a wide-ranging variety. Evergreen beech forests softly cover the hills. Southern ratas announce summer with a brilliance of red bloom, startling in dense rainforest, where shape and form lend more definition than colour, and most plants, pollinated by wind, produce flowers of muted tones. Even alpine flowers, which in most countries are vividly bright, in New Zealand are primarily whites and pale yellows.

The fauna, aside from introduced deer, rabbits, rats and the like, is restricted to birdlife, insects, lizards and the remarkable reptile, the tuatara. The only indigenous mammals are two species of bat.

The shortfall is made up by the wonderful selection of birds, ranging from the common fantail, waxeye and kingfisher to the flightless birds — the kiwi, takahe and kakapo — and the graceful waterfowl, among which the beautiful kotuku (white heron) stands out. It breeds only at Westland's Okarito Lagoon and has become one of the symbols of the burgeoning conservation movement.

South of Westland the narrow coastal flatlands disappear, and once more the work of ancient glaciers imposes on the rugged terrain. Here the deep trenches carved long ago by massive rivers of ice were flooded by the Tasman, and narrow fingers of sea probe deep inland from the coast. Milford Sound, best known of the thirteen named sounds, displays vast walls of rock rising sheer for hundreds of metres. Of these, the towering Mitre Peak captures the grandeur of scale that is so typical of the South Island.

Called sounds, these great clefts in an otherwise impregnable coast are, in fact, true fiords and compare with their counterparts in Norway.

Manapouri, Te Anau, Wakatipu, Wanaka, Hawea, Ohau, Pukaki, Tekapo, Rotoiti, Rotoroa — melodious names, enchanted with myth. These deep and ice-cold lakes, in the lee of the Alps, are the inland counterparts of the fiords. Fringed by bush, or edged by the golden tussocklands of the high country, they faithfully mirror the mountains and add to the wonder of the landscape.

Fishermen enjoy catching trout from their waters, boat tours reveal tiny beaches along their shores, and their waters nourish parched valleys. And without overly compromising their beauty, power stations utilise many of these vast reservoirs to distribute their vitality — south to the aluminium smelter, and the regional needs of Canterbury and Otago, and far away to the distant cities of the North Island.

There's one final area where water has invaded the land. The Marlborough Sounds, formed as ancient river valleys, were drowned by the melting waters of the last ice age. The Sounds balance the fiords at the opposite end of the island; yet once more a contrast is evident. Here intricacies of bays and inlets among gently rumpled hills can be confusing. What is island? What is mainland? The area is a sheltered haven for holidaymakers and boaties; and for the inter island ferries, too, Queen Charlotte Sound is a welcome refuge from the capricious seas of Cook Strait.

Names on the charts of Marlborough Sounds are pointers to stories of exploration.

One of the embellishments to the tale of Kupe's discovery of New Zealand relates his energetic pursuit of a giant octopus (wheke) across the Pacific. At Whekenui Bay he finally captured his quarry.

Captain Cook also found the Sounds in the course of his first voyage of discovery around New Zealand. He returned to the sound he named in honour of his Queen, Charlotte, several times, finding it to be then, as now, a perfect haven for rest and recreation.

French names —D'Urville Island, Croisilles Harbour — mingle with the English and Maori. The French sent several expeditions of exploration and scientific discovery to these parts, and at Akaroa, on the peninsula adjacent to Christchurch, a unique Gallic township is a continuing reminder that the English were not alone in their interest in this land.

From 1840 on, organised immigrant schemes, spawned in the comfort of England, enticed settlers to 'New Munster', the early English name for the South Island. Nelson emerged as a prosperous cathedral city, surrounded today by apple orchards, and hops and tobacco fields. The neighbouring hills have yielded valuable clays, and sunny Nelson has a high proportion of potters and craftspeople.

Dunedin and Christchurch, the other principal settlements, were both opened up by religious leaders — Presbyterians claimed Dunedin as the 'Edinburgh of the South' and Anglicans designed Christchurch to be 'the most English city outside of England'.

The contemporary cities reflect these aspirations and the orderly charm, churches, and somewhat restrained nature of their citizens contrast with their counterparts in Auckland. There lingers too a guarded reserve towards the north. For once the gold rushes of Central Otago were over, there was a marked exodus to the north, particularly to the booming new financial capital of Auckland. It was a trend that has continued, and currently less than twenty-five percent of New Zealanders dwell in the South Island.

Political solutions and economic incentives may be part of the answer to counter this imbalance. Until then the small population, the grand scale of agriculture, the high country runs, the vast wheat fields, the giant hydro projects, and the splendour of the dramatic environment, much of it within National Parks, give the South Island its unique character.

First European explorer. . .

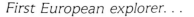

TASMAN BAY South from Stephens Island, an evening flight passes over the intricacies of Tawhitinui Reach and Croisilles Harbour. Beyond are the waters of Tasman Bay where New Zealand's first European explorer, Abel Tasman, anchored briefly in 1642. The French names of the north-west corner of the Marlborough Sounds are a legacy of Dumont D'Urville, a dedicated geographer who charted areas of the Sounds ignored by Cook.

STEPHENS ISLAND With no landing places from the sea Stephens Island at the northernmost tip of the Marlborough Sounds is a perfect sanctuary for two very special inhabitants. The Tuatara survives here in large numbers. Less numerous, but even more unique, is the tiny, pop-eyed Stephens Island frog (*Liopelma hamiltoni*), found only here and in nearby Maud Island.

99

FRENCH PASS The settlement of French Pass snuggles against the shelter of the headland. Between it and D'Urville Island is a narrow strait whose exceptionally fast tide race is well known to mariners. The most memorable navigator of French Pass has been 'Pelorus Jack', one of New Zealand's famous dolphins. For 24 years up until 1912, this Risso Dolphin greeted passing ships, delighting passengers as he played on the bow-waves.

ENDEAVOUR INLET The sheltered waters of Endeavour Inlet, the largest of many within Queen Charlotte Sound, are a paradise for sailors and launch owners, with unspoilt bays and a multitude of picnic spots.

The Sounds are a 'drowned river system'. When the ice melted at the end of the last Ice Age the rising waters flooded ancient river valleys. The hilltops became islands and peninsulas, the charming complex of the Sounds.

PICTON Picton Harbour, with placid waters deep inside the shelter of Queen Charlotte Sound, is, surprisingly, one of New Zealand's busiest ports.

Several times daily, Picton's 3,300 strong population is swollen by passengers disembarking from one of the fleet of inter-island ferries. Beside the ferries, fishing boats, yachts and charter launches tie up in the Picton Harbour. A popular excursion with visitors to the Sounds is the mailboat run to outlying homesteads.

Near the yacht basin rests the 80 year old scow, *Echo*. Romantically pretty in her fresh paint, her years of hard work are disguised by appearances. For many years this sturdy vessel, in true N.Z. scow tradition, hauled 14,000 tons of cargo annually across the Cook Strait. It was only as recently as 1965 that this fine vessel was removed from service.

MAHAU SOUND Driftwood gathers in a quiet bay on Mahau Sound. During the 1860s the valleys of the Pelorus and Rai Rivers at the southern end were cleared of their trees and dairy farms established on the cleared land.

At nearby Paradise Bay a dairy factory was for many years supplied with milk collected from farms by launch alone. It has taken a long time for roads to thread their way around the Sounds and there are still many areas reliant on water transport.

PELORUS SOUND From clear green waters a Pelorus Sound mussel farmer hauls a line laden with shellfish. Mussels, yet another of the country's fine seafoods, occur naturally on rocks below low water mark all along the coastline. Now they're being farmed commercially and lines of buoys in secluded bays mark the submerged ropes where the clinging mussels are fattening. It's a lucrative business based on sound ecology and does not interfere with traditional Maori fishing rights.

BOULDER BANK, NELSON **Port Nelson is effectively sheltered by an unusual natural breakwater, the Boulder Bank. Haulashore Island is at the southern end of the 13 km build-up of rounded stones which encloses the waters of Nelson Haven. The original entrance to Nelson Harbour was inland of Haulashore Island and it was in this vicinity that Nelson's first English immigrants stepped ashore in 1842.**

On the Boulder Bank stands New Zealand's second lighthouse, a cast-iron structure brought out from England in 1861. It guides shipping to the channel cut through the end of the breakwater in 1906.

NELSON The mid-Victorian home, Broadgreen, graces the cathedral city of Nelson. Broadgreen was built for a Mr Edmond Buxton in 1855, after the style of a Devonshire farmhouse. The soil from what was to become the cellar was mixed with straw to produce 'cob' and from this unlikely combination the gracious home was built. It is one of several historical homes in the city open to visitors.

POTTERS The crafts of New Zealand are very closely linked with the land — in form as well as material. Consider the popularity of wool and weaving, the search for form within bone, wood and stone or the melding of ancient symbolic interpretations of the land forces with those materials, the restructuring of elements to become a new substance as with glass. But it is clay that has perhaps caught the largest number of people into crafting. Pottery 'took off' under the influence of Len Castle ('Years of living in close association with bush, sea and landscape has developed in me a great respect for life and natural form'). Barry Brickell, Helen Mason and others, in the well-tried New Zealand tradition, learnt as they went and then continued to learn as they taught others what they'd figured out. The experimental beginnings of home built kilns and clay dug from the edge of roads have matured into an activity where art and craft are closely aligned. Pots have practical value or may be experiments in aesthetics and form, and many of today's potters have gained the community and cultural backing to allow them to pursue their profession full time. Nelson has built up a reputation as a centre for craftspeople and there are many potters among them. They take advantage of the top quality clays that occur locally — clays so suitable for pottery that some are exported to Australia.

The shelves of local craft shops and galleries have a wide selection of pottery available, ranging from utilitarian plates, mugs and bowls to works of pure creativity. The pictures here show potters at the Omaio Pottery, Brightwater, Nelson. Not surprisingly, the workshop is in itself a carefully crafted place.

TAKAKA RIVER The Takaka River winds its way down to Golden Bay through an isolated valley trapped between the limestone hills of Abel Tasman National Park on one side and the Tasman Mountains on the other.

A high rainfall and warm temperatures mean good grass, and first rate dairying on the river flats.

The Nelson region has some of the country's oldest rocks and an extremely varied geology. The Takaka hills have deposits of marble, nickel, asbestos and gold. During 1857 and 1858 a small gold rush around Takaka and Collingwood occurred, paralleling the first finds on the Coromandel. However today it is limestone and marble that are quarried. The former is used in cement manufacture and multi-hued Takaka Hill marble has been used in the construction of many fine buildings, such as the Nelson Cathedral and Parliament Buildings. The limestone hills have a maze of underground caverns and rivers which attract many 'pot-holers' and speleologists.

KAHUTARA RIVER The Pacific boundary of Marlborough is dominated by the Kaikoura Ranges. North of Kahutara River the rugged hills step back briefly to permit plains to skirt the Kaikoura Peninsula. Here, sheep and beef cattle take second place to dairy cows, and cheese making is an important industry.

Forest plantations...

FOREST, HANMER SPRINGS The forest plantations at Hanmer Springs, North Canterbury, date back to 1902. Convict labour planted a wide variety of species, many of which flourished, and the State Forest here has the largest number of exotic species of all the man-made plantations. The low cloud swirling through the forested valley is perhaps similar to the 'remarkable fog' which brought the shepherd, William Hones, hurrying to investigate. Thus in 1859 the first European found the hot mineral springs which had long been known to the Maoris. Nowadays, the area is a pleasant holiday area incorporating the hot pools, horse trekking, skiing, tramping and fishing.

SILVER BIRCH, HANMER In keeping with the Forestry Service's policy of making the forest available as much as possible for education and recreation, there are several fine walks through the Hanmer Springs Forest. An avenue of silver birches frames daytrippers strolling along a forest track.

The Garden City...

BOTANIC GARDENS Christchurch is justifiably known as the Garden City. From the swamp, bog and shingle of the early days have risen carefully moulded landscapes. The Botanic Gardens pictured here are part of the 200 hectare Hagley Park, Christchurch's answer to Regent's Park.

Bounded by the casual meanderings of the Avon River, the Christchurch Botanic Gardens host formal rose gardens and English woodlands, glasshouses filled with cacti, begonias, and tropical species and beds of tulips. The high standards of horticulture practised here have won far reaching acclaim for this beautiful public park.

SCOTT'S STATUE Throughout central Christchurch a medley of statues are constant reminders to the 300,000 strong population of the city's historical ties. From this corner park on the banks of the Avon River a white marble Captain Robert Falcon Scott faces representations of 'Industry' and 'Concord', perched in 1st floor niches in the Chamber of Commerce building (1887) opposite.

GODLEY STATUE John Robert Godley, the 'Founder of Canterbury' is immortalized in his statue in Cathedral Square, the heart of this very English city. In partnership with Edward Gibbon Wakefield he established the 'Canterbury Association'. They aimed for an Anglican community which would ensure the continuance of both the Church and a democratic society in the England of the South. Backed by British M.P.s and high-ranking churchmen, the Association greeted the first of the Canterbury Pilgrims at Lyttelton in 1850.

The Lyttelton site, limited by the high Port Hills, was supplanted by the present one. Here across the swampy fringes of the vast plains the symmetrical street plan was surveyed out and settlement began. Locals who can trace their roots back to the 782 immigrants of the First Four Ships proudly place laurel leaves at the base of Godley's statue each Anniversary Day.

113

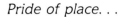
Pride of place. . .

50th JUBILEE BRASS BANDS FESTIVAL In **1845** the Band of the 58th Regiment of the Imperial Forces, affectionately known as the 'Black Cuffs' stepped ashore in Auckland and played the first brass band music in New Zealand. During the frays of the Land Wars in the North Island, the British forces were encouraged by the marches and anthems of some 13 regimental bands.

In Wellington and Auckland the army bands provided light entertainment with outdoor concerts during the weekends and the '58th' even accompanied the Auckland Choral Society's performances of the Messiah.

During the late 1860s the first civilian band formed in Alexandra, Otago, as miners from various cultural backgrounds combined their talents, instruments and tunes. By 1869 Westport, too, was sporting a band of cornets, horns, a tuba, drums, triangle and cymbals.

Music for the people was the main impetus for these bands. Yet friendly rivalries grew and in 1882 the first band competitions were held at the International Exhibition at Hagley Park in Christchurch. The rules were very relaxed: bands could have any number of players, any instruments they chose and there was no set music. A band from Timaru won first place.

The South Island developed a pride in its bands and Christchurch's Woolston Brass Band, founded in 1891, to this day is one of the country's finest.

Currently there are 450 bands in New Zealand — civic, school, Salvation Army and Highland pipe bands. Making music in disciplined groups seems to appeal to the antipodeans, thousands of whom have chosen this form of expression and entertainment. Even more derive pleasure from parades where the quickstep of the brass band brings a jaunty mood to the crowd.

It is a shame that the rather practical 'bus conductor' type of uniform has replaced the highly coloured and elegant costumes of the brass bands of the early 20th century. Sporting gay colours of green and gold, blue and white, and styles of the 'hussars' and feather-plumed hats matched with crimson trousers, those groups of men with handlebar moustaches and gleaming instruments must have cut a wonderful scene. The costuming prize is today held by the military-like groups who have formed New Zealand's unique corps of Marching Girls.

The brass bands of New Zealand are made up of amateurs and yet, still dogged by the kiwi thing of giving something a go and doing it the best, the bands have won reputations world-wide for their excellent music and have won a number of international competitions.

Novel origins...

AKAROA These cottages are typical of Akaroa, a small town on the shores of the Akaroa Harbour, an indentation on the south side of the Banks Peninsula. Unique as the only French settlement in New Zealand its origins are too novel to be easily forgotten. Romantic versions of historical fact tell of a race between the French and the British to claim sovereignty at Akaroa. However, although the picture of a race south from Russell between the ships *Britomart* and *L'Aube* is attractive, Britain's claim had been cemented in the Treaty of Waitangi while the French emigres were still en route from France.
Nonetheless 63 French people settled at Akaroa to farm. Family names, streets such as 'Rue Balgueri' and 'Rue Lavaud' and Gallic styled cottages keep the area's history alive.

BANKS PENINSULA The scene of the earliest European interest in Canterbury, Banks Peninsula drew flax traders in the 1820s, whalers in the 1830s and a party of French settlers in the 1840s.
The Peninsula has many sites and buildings of historic interest including Stoddarts Cottage dating back to 1862.

RAKAIA RIVER MOUTH The waters of the Rakaia River twine and intertwine in an intricate braid as they cross the gentle slope of the Canterbury Plain. With headwaters high in the Southern Alps the Rakaia, along with the other massive watercourses the Waimakariri and the Rangitata, carries much needed water through the thirsty plain.

At places the Rakaia is a mile wide. Here at its mouth it fans out even further creating a myriad of shingle islets. Small fishing settlements on either bank host those attracted by the excellent trout and salmon fishing.

WEST TIMARU On the rolling downs of West Timaru carefully bred flocks of sheep are fattened for export. The favoured 'Canterbury Lamb' is bred from Southdown rams and Romney ewes. Corriedales, of Lincoln-Leicester and Merino ancestry, first reared in these regions late last century, are another successful breed which gives prime export meat and long wool clips.

CANTERBURY PLAINS The kaleidoscope of colour and pattern that is the Canterbury Plains runs for 160 km from Rangiora (north of Christchurch) south to Timaru, constituting the largest level area in the country. Three vast rivers originating in the mountains and lakes of the Alps have over the centuries bought down the silt and gravel which has built up the plains. The coastal swamplands and inland tussocks have been transformed to a mixed farming region where grain and livestock are grown.

UPPER WAITOHI 25 km inland from Timaru at Upper Waitohi, the Canterbury Plains have all but gone. Here in South Canterbury lies the downland, the hummocked and valley-rifted transition between lowland and mountain.

It was not far from here that William Pearse, in 1903, flew one hundred yards (landing in a hedge) in his pioneering, farmyard-built, aeroplane. This farmer-aviator was in the air a full nine months before the Wright Brothers. His plane, constructed from bamboo, fabric and scrap metal, incorporated control flaps on the wings (ailerons) and a variable-pitch propeller directly connected to the home-made engine.

KAKANUI The market gardens at Kakanui, south of Oamaru, are intensively worked, growing a wide range of vegetables including potatoes and tomatoes in the fertile brown clay loams.
In the 1870s Kakanui had a busy port centering on the local meat cannery. Predictably, this business collapsed with the development of refrigeration.

WAINOMO LAGOON A narrow strip of shingle   separates the waters of the Wainomo Lagoon from the sea. This is a wildlife sanctuary where South Island geese come to winter.

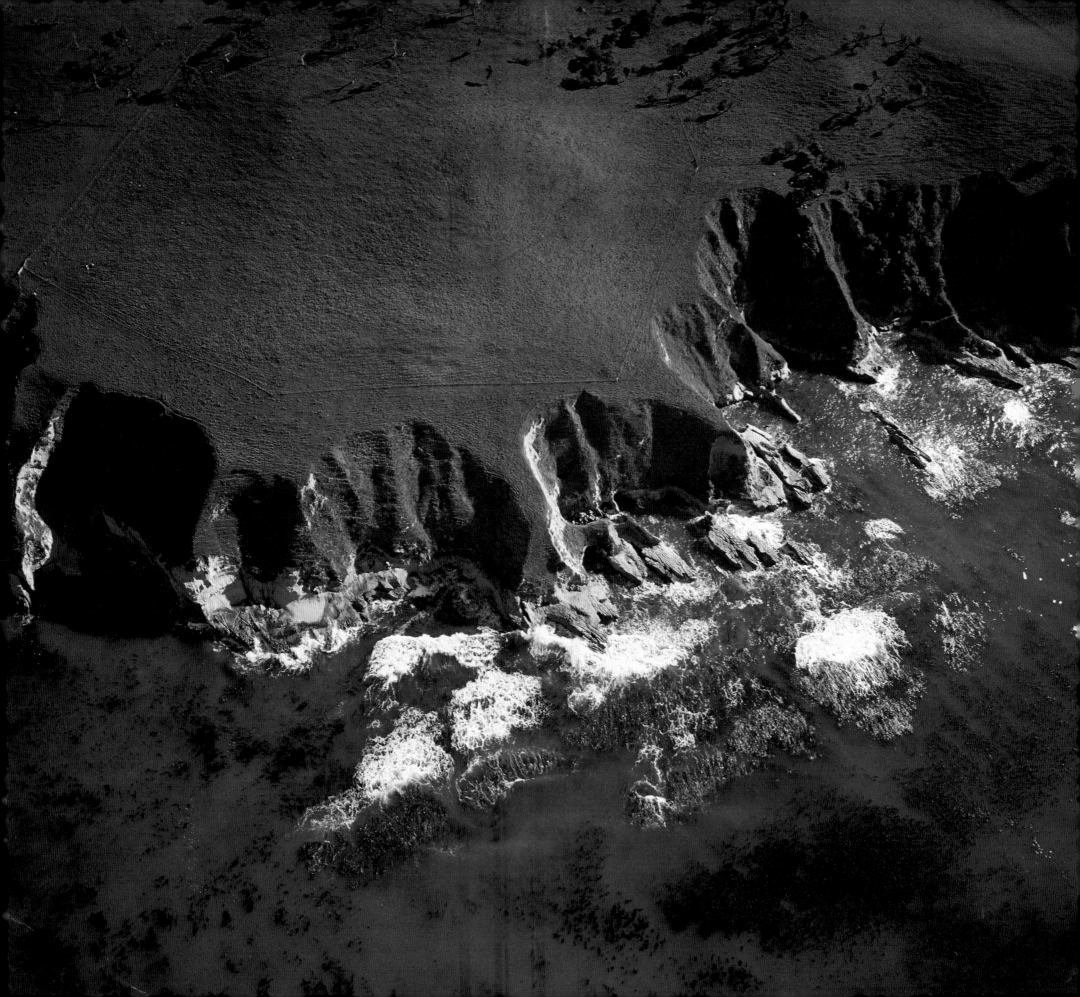

Coastal grandeur...

KARITANE Karitane is a pleasant seaside town on the south side of the Waikouaiti Estuary, with its sandy ocean beach and tidal rivers attracting holidaymakers from nearby Dunedin.

The Huriawa Peninsula (seen at the bottom of the picture) is connected to the mainland by little more than a strip of sand. As far back as the 1700s this was a precious pa site for the Ngaitahu. It had a natural spring and a landing beach nestled under the cliffs, two factors enabling a six month seige to be withstood.

123

LANARCH'S CASTLE Of all the dreams pursued in Otago's early heady days, that of W. J. Lanarch must surely rate among the most ambitious. A banker, financier and Minister of the Crown (1875-1898), Lanarch was also a romantic. His grandiose home was lavishly fashioned by foreign craftsmen from quality materials at great expense (£150,000). Styled after a Scottish baronial manor, Lanarch's Castle combines unlikely elements — colonial verandahs, a Georgian staircase, Italian marble fireplaces, a ballroom, turrets, glasshouses and stables — in a Victorian extravaganza atop the hills of the Otago Peninsula.

WAIANAKARUA Historic buildings grace the countryside. This lovely old mill house built in 1879 is now a restaurant and motel.

Victorian splendour...

DUNEDIN Sheltered by the hills of the Otago Peninsula is the slender 15km-long arm of the Otago Harbour. Around the upper reaches of this sheltered harbour nestles the Victorian splendour of Dunedin, 'the Edinburgh of the South'. The gracious and orderly nature of the town harks back to the manner with which the early Scottish settlers channelled the wealth of the Otago goldfields to produce a prospering city and commercial capital of New Zealand at a time when Wellington and Christchurch were still but shanty towns.

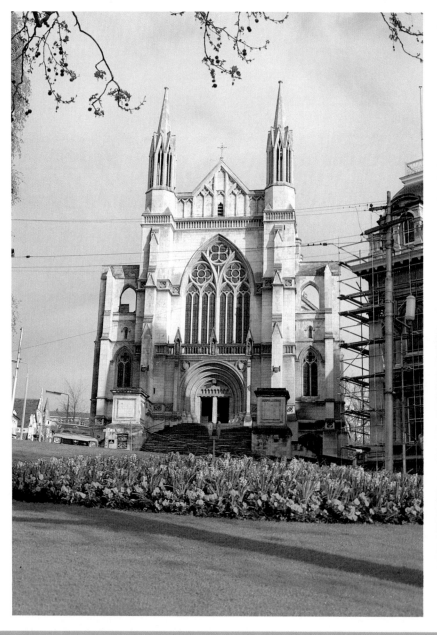

When Patrick Tuckett chose Dunedin's site in 1844 he described it as 'an ornamental and commodious site'. And although the first of the settlers found the lack of flat land tedious, the same hills and gullies have ensured an enduring charm to the residential areas. Over 400 hectares of parks and reserves including the wooded and picturesque 'Town Belt' ring the city, the result of the foresight of the early inhabitants' town planning.

The first citizens were Presbyterians from the breakaway 'Free Church of Scotland' and although Anglicans and atheist gold–diggers outnumbered them in time, the Scottish standards of hard work, orderliness, and good business endured and continue to infect the mood of the city. As too does the love of whisky — this is the only place in New Zealand where the liquor is distilled.

In brick and stone Dunedin consolidated the wealth acquired after the 1861 gold discovery at Gabriel's Gully. As the Otago Province population soared from 12,600 to over 60,000 in two short years, the city grew to become New Zealand's largest town and remained the commercial centre until the turn of the century.

The Victorian charm of the city's older public buildings is reflected in the leisurely pace of Dunedin life.

An 1860s cottage, attractive in its simplicity, catches as much attention as the grand mansions of Dunedin. The Cable House in Cumberland Street is a delightful example of an early Otago home with its high gabled roof and constrained fretwork decorating the verandah and dormer windows. Built by the Cable family in 1861 it remained in the family for 112 years before being rebuilt by the Historic Places Trust.

Otago landscape. . .

KUROW A light dusting of early snow whitens the ranges which rise steeply behind the farming district at Kurow. The name is a corruption of Kohurau, the Maori name for Mt. Bitterness, and means many mists.

OTAGO HOUSE The gold has gone from the ground but in autumn the colours of turning leaves bring a rich glow to the Otago landscape. Here more than anywhere else in New Zealand the change of season is overwhelmingly apparent as introduced deciduous trees advance through their annual cycle.

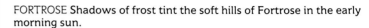

Green gold. . .

FORTROSE Shadows of frost tint the soft hills of Fortrose in the early morning sun.

Southland's vibrant pastures are very much the product of hard labour within the confines of a raw climate. The grass growing season is short, rainfall is high and sunshine hours are low. Nonetheless, the region's four freezing works slaughter 6 million lambs for the export market annually, making Southland a key contributor to the country's overseas earnings.

LAWRENCE Smooth rounded hills evocative of a Colin McCahon or Michael Smither painting are sensuous landscapes at Lawrence, Otago. Here the emerald grasses of the coastal lowlands have crept 40 kilometres inland. Typical of coastal Otago and Southland farms, the land is patchworked with ploughed fields being readied for the sowing of supplementary feed crops.

The peace of this rural scene bears no hint of the mad days during the 1860s when the gullies of Lawrence were scoured for pay dirt. The quest for gold brought men in their thousands from all over the world and Lawrence, the oldest of the goldrush towns, had a population of 11,500 in 1862, just one year after the first strike at Gabriel's Gully.

SOUTHLAND Te Waewae and Toetoe Bay are two of the three huge bays at the bottom of the South Island. Both are named after Maori chiefs whose fishing villages were situated locally. Te Waewae can be dug for the shellfish delicacy, the toheroa – usually associated with Ninety Mile Beach at the opposite end of the country. Its sands also yield small amounts of gold washed there by the Waiau River halfway along its length. Looking west, Bluecliffs Beach leads the eye to the interface between cultivated pastures and the unrestrained beginnings of Fiordland.

Behind Toetoe Bay, Lake Vincent and small waterways drain a once marshy region that fertilisers and modern farming knowledge have transformed into first class pasture.

Succulent seafood. . .

BLUFF A fiery sky lights up the houses and fishing fleet of the port of Bluff. For a limited season each year these boats brave the stormy waters of Foveaux Strait, dredging for the succulent 'Bluff' oysters that compete with toheroa and crayfish for the accolade of New Zealand's most succulent seafood.

PENGUINS Large numbers of yellow-eyed penguins inhabit the sandy bays on the seaward side of Otago Peninsula. At Penguin Beach and Sandfly Bay these charming wee creatures surf in on the waves, then preen themselves at the water's edge before toddling up the dunes to their nests among the marram grass and tussock.

The coast here has a wealth of wildlife. Seals and sealions dwell on the rocky foreshores and islets at Taiaroa Head, the spectacular royal albatross breeds in a unique colony untypically near human habitation.

Unspoiled paradise...

BLUFF HARBOUR With all of Southland's export produce of meat and wool being shipped out from here, the port of Bluff is one of New Zealand's busiest. Long a safe refuge for seafarers around the dangerous southern coasts, this bustling port has had its loading and docking facilities extended by the construction of an artificial island in mid-harbour. Bluff is also the departure point for the ferry to Stewart Island, and base for the Foveaux Strait oyster fleet.

OBAN, STEWART ISLAND The fishing village of Oban, Stewart Island's sole township, is the gateway to the unspoiled paradise of New Zealand's third largest island. The roads stop a short distance out of town – from then on walking tracks provide access to a wilderness area, as rich in beauty and wildlife as it is remote.
Three times a week the ferry, Wairua, steams the 30 km wide Foveaux Strait from Bluff, bringing supplies, mail, and a smattering of tourists, trampers and hunters. The ferry's arrival in Halfmoon Bay is a reminder of time – a commodity easily mislaid in this tranquil Antipodean outpost.

Majestic remoteness. . .

FIORDLAND NATIONAL PARK Fiordland National Park is New Zealand's largest with 1,214,000 hectares. It encompasses the majestic fiords of the remote south-western corner of the South Island, a succession of richly bushed ranges and snow-capped peaks, and the spectacular high-altitude lakes of Te Anau and Manapouri.

The magnificent scenery is the result of vast, steady earth movements and cycles which began 300-400 million years ago and culminated in glaciation during the last millenia. Vast rivers of ice plunged west directly into the sea, gouging out the sounds; east of the divide they swept into massive basins where the Park's exceptionally deep lakes have formed.

Manapouri, often claimed as the most beautiful lake of them all, means 'lake of the sorrowing heart'. Maori mythology tells of two sisters who, destitute and exhausted after wandering far from their home, wept such tears of sorrow that the mountains drew apart and caught their tears thus forming the lake. Certainly there is a feminine softness of form as the intricate shoreline wends in and out of bushed coves and past delicate beaches, and small islets.

Rainforested mountains. . .

DOUBTFUL SOUND Doubtful Sound, one of 13 named fiords in the remote south-western corner of the South Island, reaches past narrow island-clogged straits at its seaward end to penetrate the rainforested mountains of Fiordland National Park.

When the last Ice Age ended relatively recently (15,000 years ago), the rising waters flooded the deep scars left by ancient glaciers which had ground paths through the hard metamorphic gneiss, ancient rocks dating back to the earliest geological ages, to create today's fiords.

Doubtful Sound, with 160 km of coastline, cleaves its path far inland to Deep Cove where the depth of the water is too great for conventional piles and the wharf has had to be cantilevered from the steep shore.

Only recently, with roads constructed to Manapouri Power Scheme's water outfall at Deep Cove, has Doubtful Sound become accessible to anyone other than trampers and fishermen.

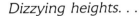
Dizzying heights. . .

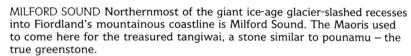

MILFORD SOUND Northernmost of the giant ice-age glacier-slashed recesses into Fiordland's mountainous coastline is Milford Sound. The Maoris used to come here for the treasured tangiwai, a stone similar to pounamu – the true greenstone.

Milford is the most accessible of all the fiords. By sea plane, walking track and road, travellers come here to wonder at the powerful forces of creation. From the depths of the sea, sheer valley walls thrust effortlessly skywards. In places the sea cliffs are 1200 metres high. A launch at the base of the Southern Wall puts the scale in perspective.

MILFORD TRACK For a limited season each summer, tramping enthusiasts vie for the opportunity to trek what has been called time and again 'the finest walk in the world'. In escorted guided tour groups or as independent 'freedom walkers' they retrace the footsteps of Quinton McKinnon, the Scotsman who discovered this overland route to Milford Sound in 1888. The 54 km walk takes from three to five days and embraces the most noteworthy aspects of Fiordland: bush, alpine splendour, and the commanding Milford Sound.

The track is always begun at the head of Lake Te Anau and the first stage is along the forested banks of the Clinton River. After climbing the dizzying heights of MacKinnon Pass, the path plunges into the Arthur Valley for the final easy section to Milford Sound.

This aerial view of MacKinnon Pass, here blocked by winter snows, looks back to the Clinton Canyon.

A sidetrip from the pass leads to the Sutherland Falls, New Zealand's highest with a drop of 580 metres. Pictured is the falls' lofty reservoir, Lake Quill, named after the first of only two climbers who have made the difficult ascent to the lake.

Spirit of adventure. . .

SPIRIT OF ADVENTURE The Spirit of Adventure reaches down the deep unpolluted waters of Doubtful Sound, undeterred by early navigator James Cook's reluctance to sail there for fear of losing wind. This graceful schooner, gifted to the youth of the nation for sail training, is usually based in Auckland but periodic circumnavigations extend the opportunity to young sailors from other ports.

FIORDLAND Two centuries ago the remote Fiordland was a hive of activity. Visits by British explorers Cook and Vancouver, and by the Spaniard, Malaspina, had produced detailed charts for many of the sounds. The reports from their naturalists of large numbers of seals were keenly received by sealers and by the turn of the 18th century, sealing gangs were busy with the first commercial exploitation of these shores.

The sealers led a rugged life which often turned into a struggle for survival when their ships failed to pick them up. One gang, rescued after 3 years, had a 'take' of 14,000 seal skins. It is hardly surprising then that after 30 years the New Zealand furseal had been slaughtered past profitable numbers.

Now protected by law, the species has recovered and seals and sealions are often seen sunning themselves on the reefs and rocky shores of Fiordland.

In Dusky Sound are the remains of New Zealand's first recorded shipwreck. In 1795 an 800 ton Indiaman sprang her seams in a mid-Tasman storm and ran for shelter at Dusky. But the *Endeavour* (not to be confused with Cook's ship of the same name) foundered in the sheltered waters. Over the years the wreck provided spare parts for many mariners but the cannons had tumbled into 20 metres of water and were beyond reach. In 1984 a salvage operation successfully hoisted the two hefty old weapons from the sea floor.

Alpine lands...

MURCHISON MOUNTAINS Bounded by the Middle and South Fiords of Lake Te Anau, soar the rugged heights of the Murchison Mountains. The Bluffs are stark against the dense beech forest.

The Murchison Mountains have been closed to the public to protect an extremely rare bird, thought to be extinct until discovered in the steep alpine tussocklands here in 1948. The takahe (*Notornis mantelli*) is a colourful blue and olive green flightless bird about the size of a hen. The Wildlife Service is also rearing takahe chicks for release elsewhere (Maud Island, Pelorus Sound) in an attempt to increase the takahe's chances of survival.

Fiordland's rainfall is among the highest in the world (well over 6,000mm — measure it in metres!) hence the magnificent forest and waterfalls that abound.

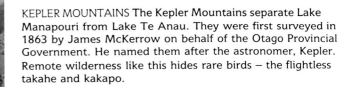

KEPLER MOUNTAINS The Kepler Mountains separate Lake Manapouri from Lake Te Anau. They were first surveyed in 1863 by James McKerrow on behalf of the Otago Provincial Government. He named them after the astronomer, Kepler. Remote wilderness like this hides rare birds – the flightless takahe and kakapo.

CASCADE RIVER From its source in the asbestos-carrying Red Hill Range, the Cascade River meanders across the Hermitage Swamp to merge with the Tasman Sea. This vast river valley, 20 km south of Jackson Bay and inaccessible by road, is the last of Westland's level ground. From here on the hills stack up relentlessly as the Southern Alpine Fault strikes the coast and the transformation to Fiordland's mountains is quickly completed.

Colours of autumn. . .

UPPER CLUTHA Once simple manpower had removed the easily gained alluvial gold, steam-driven dredges took over in the Clutha River. They scooped up the river bed and laid it down again as grey lifeless tailings and mountains of sludge, devoid of its wealth-making elements. In 1900 some 187 dredges were working the river; the last one at Alexandra ceased operation in 1963. Now the gold trail is marked, as here above Cromwell, by the burning autumn colours of poplars and willows.

ORCHARDS The Clutha Valley of Central Otago is a place of marvellous contrast. Bountiful orchards and lush grasses abruptly neighbour semi-desert wilderness, the result of low rainfall and extreme temperatures. Irrigation has wrought the transformation and it is common for water-races built by the prospectors of last century to be still in use.

Within microclimates of sheltered basins and valleys on either side of the Clutha, perfect conditions exist for fruit growing. Orchards around Alexandra specialise in stonefruit; apricots, nectarines and cherries.

APRICOTS, CROMWELL GORGE An enterprising goldminer, Joseph Tamblyn, realising that sooner or later the gold would run out, planted cherries, apricots, peaches and plum-trees at Roxburgh. He paved the way for a successful horticultural enterprise that now sees the orchards like this in the soon to be flooded Cromwell Gorge, bordering the Clutha River, supplying 80% of New Zealand's apricots.

LAKE HAYES, RESTORED STONE HOUSE The true force of a snowbound winter is yet to come down on this snug, stone-built homestead at Lake Hayes near Queenstown. To break the barren landscape and provide timber for future building needs, the early Scottish, Irish and English settlers began the tree planting which has ever since provided the autumn colours that are so much a part of modern Central Otago's identity.

LAKE HAYES, PEACOCK HOUSE This carefully restored stone house overlooking Lake Hayes is a superb example of Central Otago's early homesteads.

The landscape was treeless when the first settlers arrived but a wide selection of stone was available for building. Here in Central, mostly schists were used. The layered schists were easily split for use as building blocks.

RAFTERS, KAWARAU RIVER The Kawarau River is the only exit for the waters of Lake Wakatipu. It meanders around the Remarkables and then plunges into narrow rocky gorges. Exhilarating river trips in rafts or jet boats are offered on the rapids of the Kawarau, the Shotover and the Arrow. Most of these tours stop at old gold workings along the way to give the modern day adventurers a chance to pan for some gold.

LAKE WANAKA Rolls of hay will be welcome supplementary feed once the winter sets in. Times are changing fast. Modern farm practices even include using a helicopter in winter to pay out the feed if the snow is too thick to get a tractor out along the flats.

The summer at Lake Wanaka is warm although the waters of this snow fed lake are always cold. They offer good fishing and this along with catches of waterfowl attracted Otago Maoris up here in pre-European times during the more kindly months of the year. There were campsites at several places along Wanaka's shores and on several of the islands that grace the wanderings of this lengthy glacial watercourse.

145

Mountain pastures. . .

SHEEP, MT ASPIRING Mt Aspiring, the Matterhorn of the Southern Alps, rises splendid, serene for 3,035 metres above sea level. Seen here from the river flats adjacent to Lake Wanaka at the height of summer, it is difficult to imagine the glaciers that slide down Aspiring's highest valleys, and its winter dominance over the alpine peaks of the Mt Aspiring National Park.

SHEEP ON ROAD, QUEENSTOWN Queenstown, with ski resorts, gondolas, international hotels complete with nightclubs, scenic trips on lake steamers or jet boat rides on the Shotover — indeed all the features of one of the country's foremost tourist resorts. But all around the picturesque township lie the mountain pastures of large sheep stations. The day to day task of moving stock, shearing, dipping; the thousand and one components of producing a top-class wool clip, contrasts starkly with the jet set feel of Queenstown at the height of the season.

DEER FARM, QUEENSTOWN, As traditional markets for wool, mutton and beef become less certain for the New Zealand farmer, new agricultural enterprises are being pioneered. Deer farming, with products of venison and antler velvet, hold promise. As can be seen at this Queenstown deer farm particularly high fences are needed to keep the fleet footed deer in check. Following their introduction in the 1800s by sports minded colonists, deer multiplied rapidly everywhere in both islands. But the environmental damage was severe. Hunting and trapping red, sika, sambar and fallow deer, as well as thar and chamois, has become more than a sport. It is an environmental necessity to control these hungry browsers. Deerfarming is transforming what have been regarded as noxious wild animals into highly prized livestock.

LAKE HAWEA Lake Hawea lies parallel to Lake Wanaka, separated by steep ridges which climb rapidly to heights of up to 2000 metres. The smallest of Otago's three alpine lakes, it nonetheless is 35 km long and 8 km wide. The long, narrow and deep (300m plus) shapes of Hawea and its companions derive from their origins during the last ice age when glaciers gouged out their beds and dammed the ends with rubble.

147

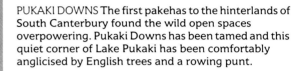

PUKAKI DOWNS The first pakehas to the hinterlands of South Canterbury found the wild open spaces overpowering. Pukaki Downs has been tamed and this quiet corner of Lake Pukaki has been comfortably anglicised by English trees and a rowing punt.

LAKE OHAU, FOG The sun rising on this fresh February morning reveals a mist hovering over the cool water of Lake Ohau. Its name means windy place — maybe in winter or later in the day. Enjoy the tranquility while it lasts.
Trout fishermen come here for rainbow and brown trout and campers and boaties also relish the charming lake as a summer spot.

CANAL, LAKE PUKAKI Throughout the South Island scenery is reflected in the waters of a myriad of lakes. Less typically, yet equally dramatically, the broad canal running for 27km between Lakes Tekapo and Pukaki, mirrors a placid summer sky.
Nearby, the 13km Pukaki-Ohau canal links the third of these vast glacial lakes into a magnificent feat of engineering, the Upper Waitaki Hydro Power Development. This complex scheme to utilise the enormous water run-offs from the Southern Alps to the west of the series of lakes — a region where over 40% of N.Z.'s ice and snow lies — was initiated in the 1950s. Now there are eight power stations in all variously sited on the canals, the outlet from Lake Ohau and further downstream on the manmade lakes at Benmore and Aviemore.

Folk hero. . .

LAKE TEKAPO The first European settlers in South Canterbury looked inland and saw ranges which they assumed to be the divide between the east and west coasts. It took one of New Zealand's folk heroes to lead them to the huge alpine basin below Lake Tekapo, now known as the Mackenzie Country.

On the great Levels Station, a vast run stretching from the sea along the valley of the Opihi River, the station manager, Mr Sidebottom, was tending to the sheep on a March day in 1855. One of his Maori shepherds, a fellow named Seventeen, arrived with the news that 1000 of the Level's flock had been stolen. Along with another shepherd, the two tracked the sheep rustler. At sunset they crossed through a pass previously assumed to go to the West Coast. At its foot they saw the culprit, James McKenzie setting up camp for the night. Without ado they rode down and seized him, only to have the Scotsman escape during a fog that came down in the night.

The tales tell of his capture in Lyttelton, his refusal to plea at his trial and his eventual pardon. After that, McKenzie disappeared without trace. The valley he revealed bears his (misspelt) name and carries today large flocks of sheep. Indeed within four years of McKenzie's capture eight runs had been established and 17,500 sheep were grazing there.

TEKAPO TOWNSHIP The bungalows of Tekapo township are austere in line. Winter snows arrive early at these heights. In the North Island May is still a time for beaches; here the seasons have already put an end to summer activities.

Maoris from coastal Canterbury settlements at Temuka and Waimate made seasonal excursions to the lake for waterfowl up until the end of the last century. But the firing of the land and the drainage of the swamps altered the natural habitat of their prey to the extent that many birds disappeared in search of a more suitable environment.

KIDS, LAKE TEKAPO Lake Tekapo is fed by two braided rivers, the Macaulay and the Godley which rise in the snowfields and glaciers of the Alps.

The glorious opaque waters, milky-turquoise in appearance, are clouded by minute particles of 'rock flour' — rock ground to a powder by the relentless ice — held in suspension.

In winter the weather will close in. The mountains will be obscured by cloud and snow will reach down to the water's edge. Then skiers will replace the swimmers and the landscape will emit a contrasting allure.

SHEEP, TEKAPO These green pastures of the Mackenzie Basin are very much the result of twentieth century applications for farming. When the ill-famed James McKenzie drove his allegedly stolen flock into this hitherto hidden valley, it was covered in tough tussock and prickly matagouri. Burning encouraged tender young shoots, and time and again the sky was darkened by smoke as easy grazing was won for the sheep.

151

CHURCH OF THE GOOD SHEPHERD, LAKE TEKAPO Perhaps the most photographed church in New Zealand, the Church of the Good Shepherd stands in charming simplicity on the southern shores of Lake Tekapo. Built as a memorial to the early runholders by their descendants in 1935, the church features a clear altar window. Elaborate stained glass work would be redundant here — the majestic peaks of Mt Cook National Park rise at the far end of Tekapo capturing the glory of creation better than any human hand.

Cloud piercer. . .

MT COOK Mt Cook set afire by the last light of a clear day. New Zealand's highest peak soars 3,764m well above its neighbours in the heart of the Southern Alps.

In 1882 an Irish mountaineer, William Green was drawn halfway round the world on the strength of a photo to attempt the first ascent of the bewitching mountain. Aorangi, true to her Maori name of 'cloud in the sky' (more commonly 'cloudpiercer') drew a storm around her peak and frustrated Green's last efforts to reach the summit. It was not until Christmas Day 1894 that the mountain was at last conquered — by three New Zealanders, Messrs Fyfe, Graham and Clarke.

Alpine world. . .

MT COOK Mt. Cook is but one among many majestic, snow mantled peaks. Here in the Mount Cook National Park hundreds of mountains rise above 2,500 metres. This alpine world is both a challenge to sportsmen — mountaineers, skiers, trampers — and a delight to sightseers.

Heart of the area is the Mt. Cook village where, from the comfortable accommodation of the Hermitage Hotel and a variety of hostels, visitors strike out on a wide range of activities.

Summer months are ideal for experienced climbers to tackle the heights and passes of Mt Cook and the numerous neighbouring glaciers and mountains are challenging training grounds.
Less exacting day walks in the Hooker and Tasman Valleys offer panoramic views of the Southern Alps.

Symbol of the warm months is the 'Mt Cook Lily'. Incorrectly named by early colonists who were inclined to call any white flower a lily, this perennial herb is really a giant buttercup. In keeping with the predominant whites and yellows of New Zealand's alpine flowers, Ranunculus lyallii surrounds a yellow centre with wax-white petals.

River of ice. . .

FRANZ JOSEPH GLACIER Ka Roimata-o-Hine-hukatere the Maoris called this vast river of ice which plunges 2,400 metres in altitude from the vast neve high in the Southern Alps to the rainforested coast, stopping abruptly in a cliff-face of frozen water.

The name means the 'Tears of the Avalanch Girl'. The mountain-dwelling maiden Hine-hukatere was to marry Wawe, a man of the coastal plains. Wawe was determined to overcome his fear of the mountains which his future wife loved. One day he went climbing with her. He slipped and fell to his death. Hine-hukatere was filled with grief and her tears filled the valley where Wawe lay. The gods transformed them into the river of ice which today is known as the Franz Joseph Glacier.

Access to the constantly changing ice cliffs at the terminal face is by car or walking track.

Although the 12 km glacier 'rushes' down its steep path from the permanent snowfields on the slopes of Mt Cook and Mt Tasman at a rate of 1-5 metres daily, the terminal face is actually gradually retreating.

The milky waters of the Waiho River explode into view from the base of the glacier and cleave a path through the morainic debris that litters the wide valley. Waiho translates as 'Smoky Waters', a reference to the mist that often lingers above it as warm air meets icy water.

156

Unique glaciers. . .

FOX GLACIER The advance and retreat of the Fox Glacier is marked by the progress of the vegetation and by the distinct piles of gravel and moraine along the valley.

The Fox River, milky in appearance, is clouded by fine particles of rock flour, produced as the glacier grinds its way towards the sea. The West Coast glaciers were first explored by an Austrian, Julius von Haast. The Franz Joseph he named after the Austrian emperor and the Fox, renamed since after one of N.Z.'s Premiers, he called Albert. Both glaciers lie within the 88,629 hectares of Westland National Park, a reserve that extends from the Tasman Coast to the peaks of the divide, where it meets the Mt Cook National Park. In the continually snowbound heights more glaciers are to be found. But the Fox and Franz Joseph are unique, falling as they do from permanent snowfields to terminate at low altitudes just 16 km from the coast and within reach of ferns and rainforest.

158

Ancient mountains. . .

MT TASMAN A break in the clouds reveals the magnificent Mt Tasman, New Zealand's second highest peak (3498m). The mountain's year-round snowfields feed the Fox Glacier which, as recently as 14,000 years ago, reached right down to Gillespies Beach.

Mt Tasman is one of fifty peaks in the Southern Alps which rise above the permanent snowline. These ancient mountains of the Southern Alps were thrust up by massive folding and faulting of the earth's crust five million years ago. They border the 560 km-long Alpine Fault which runs the length of the South Island, from Milford Sound to Marlborough.

DRIFTWOOD In South Westland the virgin forests of rimu (red pine) reach down to the beaches. Stunted by the weather, these are spindly counterparts of the North Island rimus. Along with kahikatea (white pine) and beech, these trees are milled from several State Forests in Westland. This has been the source of some dispute between industry and conservationists, especially at Okarito. Okarito lagoon is the only known nesting place of kotuku, the white heron, and it is feared logging there would disrupt this rare bird's habitat.

Rugged coastline...

WEST COAST RIVERS On the near-deserted reaches of the South
Westland coast, four of many mighty rivers — the Paringa,
Waita, Haast and Waiatoto — hesitate behind shifting sandbars
before merging with salty Tasman breakers.
In this region where rainfall averages 5,000mm yearly, swollen
rivers and luxuriant temperate forests typify the landscape.

Scenic Reserve. . .

LAKE KANIERE Westland is water: as rain, fast-flowing rivers, waterfalls and tranquil lakes, snow, glaciers and, of course, sea. The reserve at Lake Kaniere is a popular spot for the Hokitika and Greymouth locals to picnic and holiday. Bushwalks lead visitors through a canopy of tree ferns and native podocarps — matai, kahikatea, rimu. The Dorothy Falls wash over moss-covered rocks on the north-eastern side of the Lake.

The 'Coasters'...

KNIGHTS POINT Melodramatically named after one of the Haast Road's surveyor's dogs, Knights Point is a superb corner of Westland. The verdant rainforest plunges down to the Tasman where sands fringe the land's edge and seals bask on the rocks.

The relaxing drive over the Haast Road bears nothing of the difficulties of roadbuilding at this very outpost of the Antipodes. On the day in 1965 that the highway opened, pouring rain brought down huge slips and promptly closed it again.

GREIGS State Highway 6 winds down the coast from Westport, threading its way along the narrow shelf between the sea and the Paparoa Ranges. Here it passes through Greigs, one of a number of small coastal settlements. From their unassuming homes step the 'Coasters', a rough and ready breed, independent and full of humour, fertile inspiration for anyone wanting to define a 'real' New Zealander.

Pancake attractions. . .

PUNAKAIKI Punakaiki is one of the most attractive spots on the Coast. Its beach is bordered by luxuriant bush and the fascinating Pancake Rocks out on Dolomite Point demand attention. Waves have washed away the softest sediments of the limestone, creating this uniquely stratified attraction. Today the weather is near perfect. But should the wind build up an incoming tide, the water will rumble its way along intricate subterranean passages and burst forth like a geyser from one of the many natural blowholes.

World heritage. . .

ARTIST The wild rocky coastline is broken by sandy coves trimmed with flax and cabbage trees.

Contrary to popular belief, the climate of the West Coast is mild, influenced by a warm sea current flowing along the coast. Mention rain, though, and the West Coast takes the prize for wetness. Blocked by the mountains of the Southern Alps, rain-laden air blows in from the Tasman Sea, cools and pours it in bucketfuls. The wonderful rain forests of the Coast thrive in these conditions.

This part of New Zealand to the west of the Alps is one of the least-spoiled areas of New Zealand and as such is a delight for artist and travellers alike.

BUSH, PORARARI Limestone outcrops break the bushline near the Porarari River, inland from Punakaiki. Bracken fern threatens to crowd back in on land cleared for farming. With less than 10% of the rugged Coast suitable for agriculture and with conservationists winning increasing support for the maintenance of indigenous forests as natural resources, the unique forests of the South Island may have a future. 60 million isolated years in the making, they are very much a world heritage.

PERPENDICULAR POINT Dwarfed by scale, Perpendicular Point does not appear to be much of a barrier to the modern traveller. But hazard it was to those journeying down the coast in early times. The Maoris scaled the 50 metre cliff with the aid of rata vine ladders. In 1865 the Nelson Provincial Government generously replaced this with a chain! Miners travelling to the goldfields further south pushed branches through the links to make a rough and ready ladder. Finally a track was hewn out of the cliff face and now cars on the sealed highway cross the problematic terrain with barely so much as a by your leave.

Ghost town. . .

DENNISTON **North of Westport, atop a 600m high plateau, are the coal mining ghost towns. Denniston is one of these. In its heyday at the turn of the century Denniston's population neared 1000 and the town had all the amenities — 5 hotels, 3 stores, a butcher, baker and halls and a hospital — even a tennis court and a swimming pool. But the howling winds, constant rains and low clouds that kept its inhabitants, in the times of poor transportation, living close to their work in the coal mines, were also responsible in the end for driving them down the twisting road to kinder conditions at sea level. Three of the original inhabitants have endured the unkind weather, and have been joined of late by several 'alternative lifestyle' craftsmen. Meantime the coalfield, named after its discoverer, R.B. Denniston, continues to be worked by 40 commuting miners who extract 1,000 tonnes weekly.**

One of the features of the old Denniston was the Incline. Rusty track and twisted timbers are pitiful relics of the world's 'steepest, self-acting incline railway'. For 87 years full coal cars rumbled down the steep bluff to the railway below providing, at the same time, the impetus for empty cars to be hauled back up to the Denniston mine.

Organised excursions offer tours of the underground mine and the famous Incline.

Sea harvest...

FISHING BOATS, WESTPORT The West Coast of the South Island, buffeted by the prevailing westerly weather, offers shipping only two ports of refuge. At both Westport (seen here) and Greymouth, harbours have been fashioned by building breakwaters at the edge of rivermouths. The Westport fishing fleet, benefiting from support from the Fishing Industry Board, catches albacore tuna for an expanding tuna industry. The trolling rigs can be seen on either side of the vessels. At night, bright lights offshore indicate the presence of Japanese squid fishermen who compete for the sea's harvest wealth.

GREYMOUTH TRAIN STATION The spruced up buildings of the Greymouth railway station are typical of an era in New Zealand when rail transport was king.

Cargoes of timber, coal and to a lesser extent, agricultural products are hauled from Greymouth across the only track braving the rigours of the Southern Alps. Carriages must be pulled by electric engine through the 8 km long Otira Tunnel which has been forced beneath Arthur's Pass at an incline of 1 in 33, before running down the Waimakariri River gorge onto the Canterbury Plains.

An interesting trip from Greymouth lasting less than two hours, is the miner's train up to Rewanui. The line winds its way through fine scenery and crosses Coal Creek several times before reaching the coalmine.

In all the line reaches from Seddonville down to Ross, less than a quarter of the West Coast — hardly surprising when one considers the terrain!

COALCARS, WESTPORT When the rush for gold died away, large reserves of high quality bitumous coal in the Paparoa Ranges behind Westport offered up a second extractive industry. Coal has been mined so long from the open cast and pit mines of the West Coast that the two are always associated together.

Bitumous coal burns very hot which makes it eminently suitable for industrial use. At Cape Foulwind, a short distance south of Westport, this energy is put to work with local limestone to produce cement at one of the country's leading cement works.

Both coal and cement are shipped out from Westport — road access to the Buller region of New Zealand is across the formidable mountainous backbone of the South Island and there is only one rail link with the East Coast, far away through Arthur's Pass.

HEAPHY RIVER Further north from Charleston, where the Heaphy River emerges from the beech forests of the Buller region, a wreck near the river heads is further testimony to the tempestuousness of the West Coast in winter. Even with modern navigational aids, many fishing vessels have been lost in stormy weather along the coast between Westport and Nelson.

NORTH KARAMEA COAST Kohaihai Bluff, a stark silhouette at the northern end of the Karamea coast, is the tricky final stage of the famous Heaphy Track. Sadly, there have been fatalities here as walkers have sought to complete their walk from Golden Bay.
At Karamea the mountains ease back from the coast and on the swampy pakihi lands an interesting experiment has been taking place. Farmers have co-operated with conservationists to formulate an environmentally balanced plan whereby some land is drained for farming while the rest remains as wetland.

CHARLESTON A huddle of baches and a single hotel impart little hint of the time when gold brought prosperity and a hundred hotels lined Charleston's main street. Nor does the bay made shallow by tailings from the mines look like the thriving port it was when Captain Charles Bonner negotiated his vessel in during winter gales to bring desperately needed provisions to the township. The mining town became 'Charlie's Town' out of gratitude.

FAREWELL SPIT The sandbar known as Farewell Spit sweeps north from the tip of
the South Island, to the isolated lighthouse far out in the Golden Bay.